Richard Hell

What Just Happened

WITH IMAGES BY CHRISTOPHER WOOL

Winter Editions, 2023

TABLE OF CONTENTS

- 11 WHEN, IN THE PAST
- 12 SUPERFLY
- 13 ODE
- 14 POEM
- 15 THE SOULS
- 17 ABOUT
- 18 AS I STROLLED
- 19 NOW GONE
- 20 PSYCHAL ANECDOTES *or* CYCLE ANNIE ("I heard her call my name")
- 22 LOVE LETTER
- 23 BECAUSE
- 24 SUNLIT BRICK WALL OUT THE WINDOW
- 24 META DESPAIR
- 24 MASS WARPS SPACE
- 25 I'M AFRAID
- 27 POST-ANTERIOR
- 29 A BEING
- 30 WHEN I TRY TO THINK
- 31 POETS
- 32 SLUGGISH
- 33 ONE THING LEADS TO ANOTHER
- 35 CONFESSION
- 36 AFTER RIMBAUD
- 36 TO PERCEIVE IS TO READ *or* LESSNESS
- 37 THE WORDS
- 45 DRAWN
- 46 PAST IS PAST
- 49 REFLECTION
- 50 MY APARTMENT
- 51 UNABLE

53	BILL KNOTT READING
55	CONSOLATION
56	MUMBLES
58	IT'S EASY TO FORGET
59	ANNUNCIATION
61	UNTITLED
63	ASSERTION
64	THE THING
66	COMPLETE FRAGMENTS
68	ADVANCED AGE
69	IDIOSYNCRASY
70	IT'S THE OBLIVION
71	POEM
72	CONTINUATION
77	FALLING ASLEEP
107	CHRONICLE
143	Acknowledgments

What Just Happened

poems

images by Christopher Wool

The day lives us and in exchange / We it
—*James Schuyler, "Hymn to Life"*

WHEN, IN THE PAST

When, in the past, my childhood
bedroom and balloon
not merely the familiar
celebratory toy, nor verb, nor basket carrier
but the relative of baleen
that "flexible, horny" substance
once used as corset stays
wherein I was made
to stay come bedtime
and wherefrom I gazed
out the window on days
so long that sunlight
lingered after bedtime
                           far
away a dog whaled.

SUPERFLY

I write better poems than anyone
and the way you can tell is
by attending the tiny hairs
until love.
People
say "love." Its most general
definition would be ego
dissolved by reality, which is also
possibly why it gets paired
with death. Flies have hair
and are named for their most conspicuous
property. "I heard a Fly buzz
— when I died — "
Buzz means fly close. Love, Richard

ODE

I'd like to write an ode to gin.
I'd want it to resemble its subject
in the form I'm taking it, being two
parts London dry to one part dry vermouth
with a couple big glugs of olive brine
in a classic cone on stem martini glass
all being icy cold, the
mixture drained over a big green
crunchy Bella di Cerignola olive
circa dusk
to ease my way to nighttime
with the goddess Judy Woodruff
reporting Trump pandemic news.

POEM

Coming upon the word
"I" in a Bill Knott poem
I felt him still alive.
I've always thought the words
"Bill Knott" aren't quite right
—as good as they may be
they are not him to me, but that
"I" is the one I just felt
him being there in now.

THE SOULS

I like the "souls" of the poets I love
more than I like their poems.
It's as if the poems roughly
correspond to their author's
being, and I'm temporarily
rescued by how my own
(being) is arranged to more
closely resemble theirs as I read.

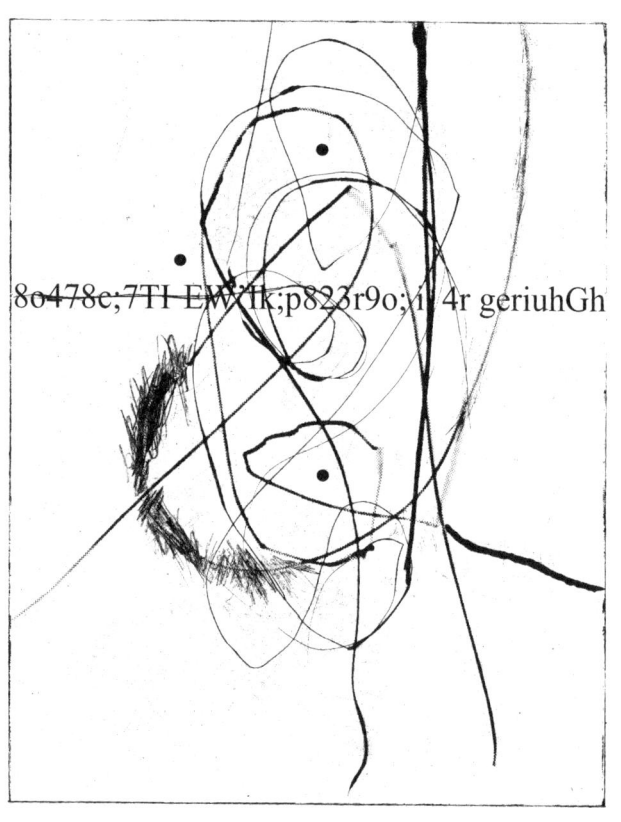

ABOUT

Something there is about
the (very small amount of) information
upon which we base our thoughts
that Bruce Nauman breaches.

AS I STROLLED

      As I strolled out inside
       protective reality
                      sunlight performed
the metaphysics of Duchamp, and then
        was perforated by birds
                         a lollipop the graphic
    and revelation-triggers like art
              forms of noise and flare from
        right through the amber, azure
              and horrible pistol
                      barrel children
     slaps or
    sometimes entrees to
death by police. Lice, lettuce, class.
                        An injured sound
    the flare of a leaf enlarging grief
        preoccupations (chess, sex, art, amusement)
   fundamentally knuckle
          but to Mallarmé was
sand struck mental stacks that reached to
                beauty or its means an element
    of their visual appeal

              or actually beyond.

NOW GONE

Sometimes it feels like this moment
is what I'll see when I am dying. Like
reverse déjà vu. Any
moment the subject of everything, almost
like a gift from nothingness, inducing
gratitude for consciousness, as when
one receives percipient praise, as the truth
of being alive. Something
you notice for the first time again, something
common, but that you notice
and then you're gone. Say, you
look up and there's the familiar window
and there is nothing to it
except that it's what's there
and you are privy to it greeting you, now gone.

PSYCHAL ANECDOTES *or* CYCLE ANNIE
("I heard her call my name")

How much does the world
have in common with the rest
of the universe? Is it its expression
or its affliction? I guess what I want
to know is whether a paradise where
dualities cease to be
is possible or does
consciousness eliminate the possibility?
Classically, poems are dictated from
without through the poet, and that occurs
but they can be arrived at
by deliberation too.
The poem says something simple or
perhaps logically opaque
in such an engaging way that one
hardly notices or cares what might
be otherwise meant.
From the engineer's seat
of a speeding train is observed
to the right a pink piglet or naked
infant child scrambling
out the window into the landscape.

I want to be named Pierre Klossowski or Raphael Rubinstein

and then my mind split open

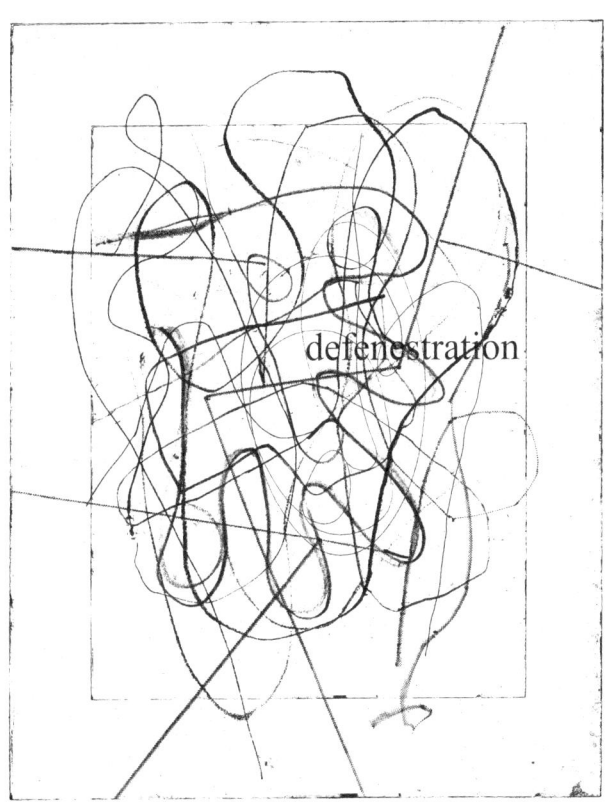

LOVE LETTER

Is anyone immune
to love letters? Maybe Noam
Chomsky. He seems mature.
Not me; I like
to be worshipped.
It's an act of faith
a love letter. I'll take it over
prayer any day—at least
you can interact with the lover
though there will probably be a lot
of frustration and humiliation
as with a deity.
What comes first, love or
sex? It's a dead heat.

BECAUSE

for Katherine

> They wandered through the hand in hand.
> —Bill Knott, "Untitled ('They wandered [...]')"

The reasons I like to be held by you
are like paint-by-number results
your touch speaks to make me
what I'm spoken by it
and I understand that
physically, as
physicality is all
and everything
the way that an excited
poet once claimed to read Chinese
ideograms sans prior knowledge
although in our case it's true
you, speechless, remove
all my unknown by touch
and I happy
then become, because
it's you and no one else who does.

SUNLIT BRICK WALL OUT THE WINDOW

I thought I was smelling the bricks but I was seeing them.

META DESPAIR

Conversational free verse of
thought more than sensation.*

---

*Despair is a sin it's said; in Christianity the one that's not forgiven.**

**That's the voice of claimed authority, but in fact God isn't hopeful.

MASS WARPS SPACE

The world is big enough to make me this heavy.

I'M AFRAID

I sought an image that
would precipitate a certain
state, a feeling
identified with the effects
of poetry.
I'm afraid of the middle
of the ocean in a way
I can fairly well suppress
but the view from lying alone
and unprotected in an
encircling horizon of sea
was the image that came.
Maybe that's in line
with Rilke's that beauty
is nothing but the beginning
of terror or Burke's
that the sublime
is formed of same
or say Dennis Cooper
but it's the ocean
as a circle with no edge
in which I'm isolated
that scares me. But
any creature in isolation
will do for such a situation
of fresh reality,
especially, in that case, if one
effectively evokes a feature
or two: say a hair

or tooth or eye or
simply symmetry
the way of William
Blake, Elizabeth Bishop or
Marianne Moore.
And then there are
the paintings. "Las Meninas"
which above all stops
time. Can "Blue Poles"
be called an image?
Poets often love the surrealists
especially de Chirico and
Joseph Cornell and painterly
and figurative images of the lone
like Morandi and Hopper.
I favor images
that mutate in only the way
that words can enable.
But none of these are what I mean
but being alone at sea.

POST-ANTERIOR

We are ants rubbing our ant
ennae together; nothing
wrong with that—ants
have the dignity of us—and
the world
thus engendered
by beings transmitting
information includes
this poem and everything
else. Does engendering involve
determination of gender? No
it's simply about the act
of generation. Shall it
be male or female in the tub?
Tub is but backwards, and but
is almost butt, which is
a person's ass. This
is one way to get from ants
to anal sex, with you.

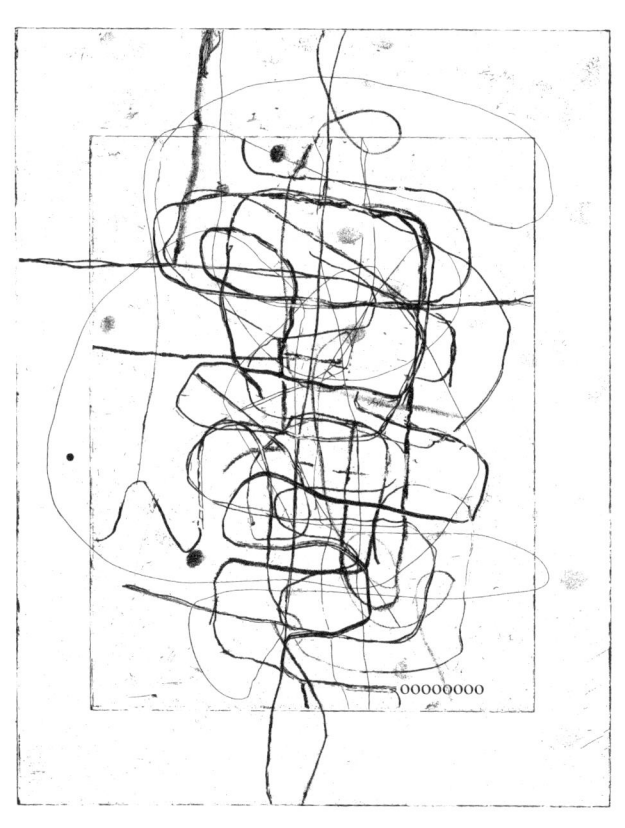

A BEING

A being like a
ball of aluminum-foil light
and thoughts are
bugs buzzing around it
reminded me of when
I turned
and saw a wild turkey
outside sporting that dangling
loose feather
clump at its chest, and there
was its pale blue and bubble-gum
pink
warty head and wattled neck
defiant snood and as-if-softly
-moaning, dark semi-iridescent
brown feathers, but most notably the
way it was just like me but better
for not being
able to need to know it.

WHEN I TRY TO THINK

When I try to think
of a random word, it's
often toe, corn or train. Corn
most often I think. The
ubiquity of corn. Turkey,
cranium, target, balls. Bang.
Is bang a word? Sheelagh
once looked at me quizzically
and asked, "Are penguins birds?"
She loved and studied
birds, but was really
stumped for a moment. I
knew just how she felt. It
gave me joy. She did.

POETS

The odd thing is how
poets hope to have
their works expose
all that time forgot.
I didn't write that line; it
made me do it: what
I meant to say is that
what poets hope to have
their writing do is somehow
trick into being
all that time forgot. It
happened again. What
I meant to remark upon is how
poets hope in their works
to let pour in what one's
habits of perception
and practical filters of biology
had walled off. I'm sacred now.
I mean scared.

SLUGGISH

When I see in dreams people
I've known who died
I sometimes understand
that they're dead and sometimes
don't, or not consciously—whatever
consciously means in a dream.
Sometimes their faces seem
bruised or lumpy in places
though it isn't really visible
as if shadow and light
could be confused.
I tend to ask them questions.
They never say much. I'm always
surprised they're so quiet.
They seem preoccupied.
On awakening
I feel sad but transported
in a maybe childish
slightly bewildered, but proud
voluptuous way, mostly
grateful to have been able to be again
with the one who'd died.
What were they thinking as we spoke?
They weren't thinking; they were dead.
It was a dream. This is
what they were thinking.

ONE THING LEADS TO ANOTHER

> Hollow portals of solid appearance
> —*Ted Berrigan, sonnet XXXIV*

I may not be mentally healthy
the metal struts and rods
within the thing like de Chirico
the name-word that arose as them
all airy amid the skeletal
metallic, and an r, o
recalling now a retrospective
of his I saw in Milan. I was
enthralled, could become
his monk I thought, whose paintings
I hadn't paid so much attention
to before, had thought
illustrative or literary.
It wasn't the familiar ones,
which were a youthful brief series
(later multiplied by his own
copies of them) but
the entire life and life's worth.
It all seems like
the descriptions puzzlers
propose of how the universe
behaves at last: black holes and rabbit
holes and worm holes: everything
empty while threshold.
Everything one sees or thinks, a hole.
It reminds me of something
I read about the identification

of God with nothing, but
I can't remember what it was.
The band Hole once played
a version of my song "Time" live.
Richard Prince's "wild history" is
a compendium of holes.
Marcel Duchamp's life's work too.
Holes of wit holding
or witholding
holding
holes holes holes

CONFESSION

I hate and fear
sentimentality
but I have to admit
that when I think
of the beauty
of the inside
of my eyelids
it almost
makes me cry.

AFTER RIMBAUD

Everything is something else.

TO PERCEIVE IS TO READ *or* LESSNESS

It's not that everything
speaks, but that we can
only perceive a thing
as signifying, here
in our mocking
remove from meaning
lessness.

THE WORDS

The words stumble and flow
out from the mental dark, sometimes
slowly, others rushed. They
aren't always made of alphabet letters
either; instead, they're made of phenomena now
language-limited, such as cars crashing
into each other—a 1958 Plymouth Belvedere
the Lucas Cranach
Venus with her complaining son
bee-bitten Cupid. But I'm losing my original
impulse: they shift or appear
from the hole, transporting
me into the future that's past and
I hear my mother speaking when she
was twenty-nine and I was four. Not
speaking but imagined speaking. She
had a pretty, fluty-oboish voice, and would never be mean.
Though I did drive her one time in my teens to
say she was glad my father was dead so
that he couldn't see what I'd become. I
was so indifferent at that point that
I felt triumphant to have elicited
enough frustration that she'd try
to be mean. I'd won—as I can't
deny I still do feel to a degree.
It feels like a melody against my skin I can't
identify except this, tracing
me with themselves to her, when our
relationship was still fresh, sixty-six years ago.

Now she's dead. But less so than I might think. The
words continue as summoned, almost like a spider's filament
immobilizing prey: pray, the way a mantis is lichened
licked and Kittled, bit, dis
tended, clicked, clopped, socked, sick, tock, pick, wok, walk
block, tip, top, frock, stop, block, wack. Pray
tell. Columns
of ants enacting epics, oceans
scientific laboratories in which Jerry (Lewis) toils. But
I walk out, affronted at *The Bellboy* when I was ten and
felt a surprising, proud, if lonely maturity
in discovering I might be moved to walk
out of a movie, something
I would never have imagined possible. But
it's my mother I was mentioning. Now that she's
dead. I realize I hardly ever thought about her
when she was alive, despite the inevitability that
she had a lot to do with my make-up and
its absence, that she must have meant
everything to me when I was three
and even five, maybe. I don't feel guilty about it though.
Being a parent means no expectation of a return
from the recipient of your genes and some
form of attention, just like the act of giving someone
something unsolicited means no... But
we know how to integrate yes and no: Coleridge's
favorite proverb was "Extremes meet," I was
slightly irked to discover, since I liked feeling that
I'd defined myself to a degree by the recognition
on my own of that hard-won insight, but then
why do they call it "recognition"?
It was already known. I remember

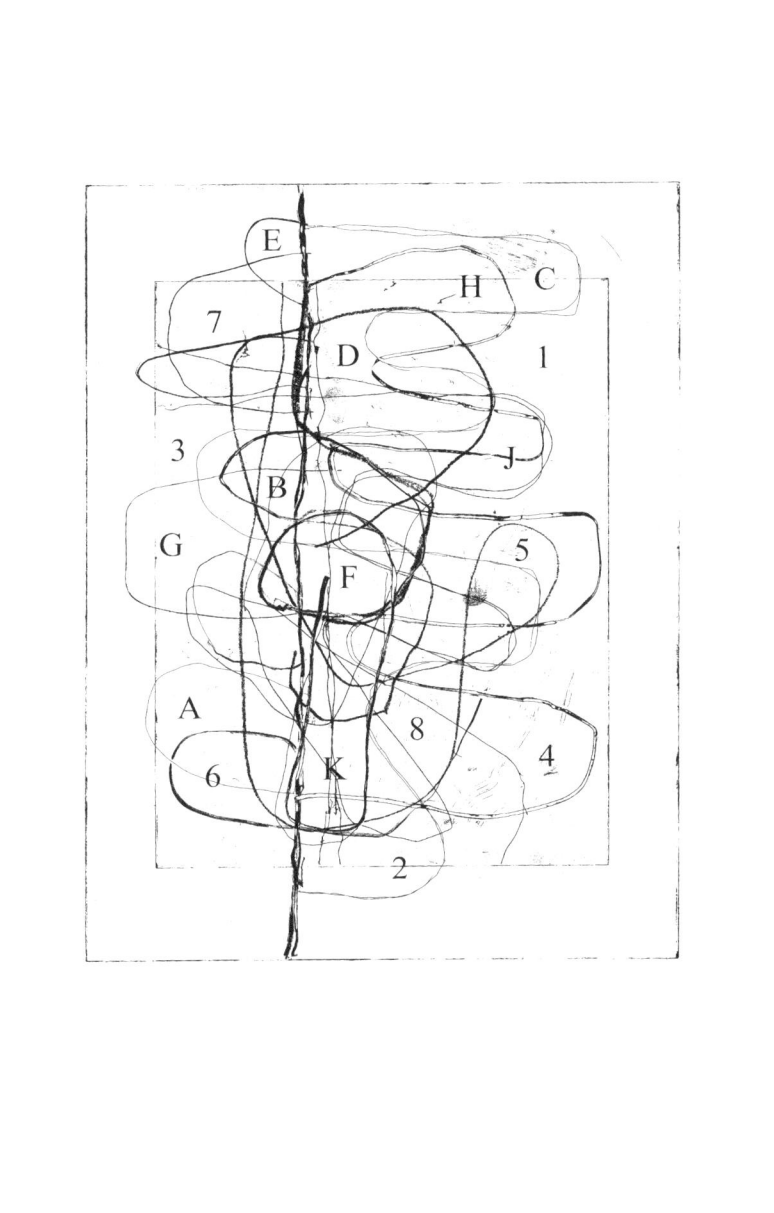

what it was like as an adult to visit her,
the ugly humility of it, the inescapable
realization that when there I was no longer
myself, but the person who deserved to be ashamed.
But that wasn't her fault. On the contrary.
She was a better person than me. She
finally made me cry when she was
crushed and helplessly unforgiving about how
I destroyed my marriage to a person we both loved.
She wanted so much not to be mean, even then
but she lost control temporarily. It's occurred to me before
that artists whose defiant transgressions I admire and
even envy, like Dennis Cooper, Kathy Acker, William
Burroughs, Bataille, Houellebecq, are people who
hated their parents, without exception (Bataille apparently
masturbated at his mother's corpse).
That was an odd perception. Their bitter bravery
and disillusion, kind and bitchy
were born of hurt feelings and loneliness. It's
just more evidence that our ideas are emotions, not
truths about reality. Which is kind of depressing.
I want the truth about reality. I suppose it's the wrong question.
I remember how affronted I was at age fourteen or fifteen
that she would take either credit or blame for me. Who
did she think she was? Parenthood of poets is especially
thankless. No question she was reserved though. She
didn't show or express emotion much, which isn't to say
she wasn't empathetic; she was. And heavily
active in support especially of civil rights and
feminism, not in regard to theory but practice.
How did this poem end up being about my mother?
I have always been embarrassed to acknowledge

I even had one. Typically for me, it took her death
to make me wonder what she meant or means to me
which isn't to say it was a whole lot. I've always
been confused about family. People think it's so
important. Why would it be more important than
your good friends? I've had various theories
about that—that it's a social test
of how well you can treat people you must
associate with, but with whom you have
little in common, for instance. Now I'm grateful
that I have my family as friends that have lasted longer
than other friendships. My house was dark and quiet
often when I came home from school. She
was at work. It depressed me, the empty
house. I remember how much I loved
the hobby shop where I could get plastic models
the most compelling of which were birds
a robin, a cardinal, a Baltimore oriole. Airplanes
and ships had their appeal, and I made some of those too
but they weren't birds. Birds birds birds birds birds
I wish poets talked more about birds. Birds are
the most enthralling unknown, way more
so than fingernails. My mother didn't use fingernail
polish. She wasn't very interested in appearances
but rather kindness and learning.
I didn't believe in anything, was my problem
and I still don't, though I would if I could
except maybe that art is interesting.
I like it when science and art intersect, for instance
in the way that the most pleasing and magisterial
lines of literature have the most vowel sounds in them
as first deduced when considering why

ia·yfPjtp8U-y.f

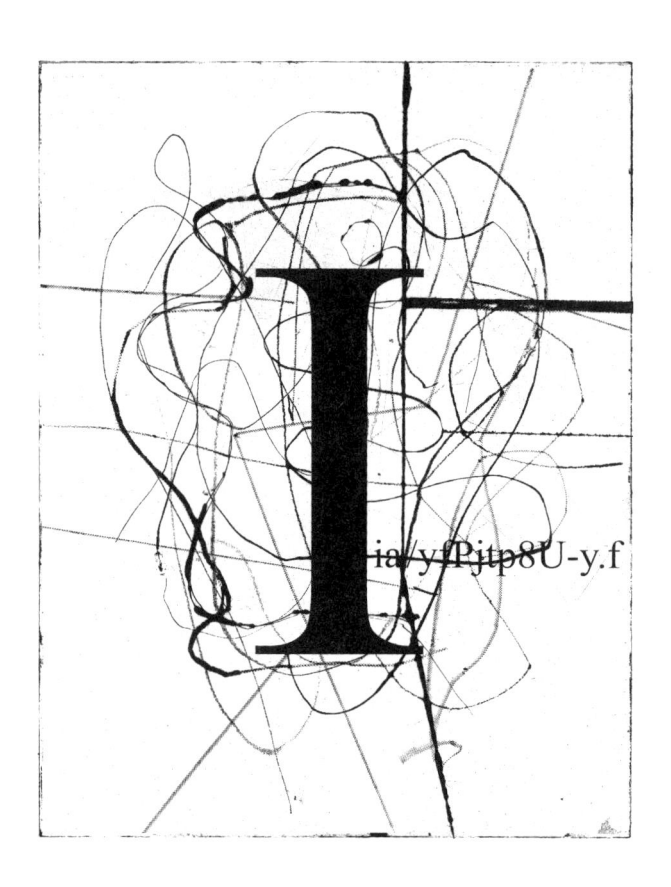

the mundane instruction to "raise
high the roofbeam, carpenters" has
the power it does. It's only because
of how it sounds. Variety of vowellings. Syntax
too, I guess. Alliteration and iambs. In other
instances pararhymes, half rhymes, colors evoked
like "the force that through
the green fuse drives the flower," or "The earth
makes a sound as of sighs and the last
drops fall," or "into the fathomless blue
of the eyes of the prides of peacocks, where
the moon rose, rosy as mother-of-pearl,
bones like the fleshless feet of peacocks danced" ("and
who am I to assign a character to the facts,
o most affable reader?") All of which lines
I've quoted here I notice now describe
nature, which is interesting, especially as
the other candidate occurring to me
did as well: "Peering
down into the water where the morning
sun fashioned wheels of light, coronets,"
etc. That's probably not a coincidence.
My mother would like that I think
and care about these things. "Kingfisher,
catch fire," you know. But it wouldn't
have compensated for my moral deficiencies
as well it shouldn't, I suppose. But
people can't do much about themselves that they
haven't been designated to by powers they don't control.
We're puppets. Apples that falling feel we've jumped,
as Spinoza put it and who's to say otherwise—but
how far from the tree?

Is that too clever? I'm going to leave it.
My mother wrote some poems too. She taught
students to interact with Emily Dickinson
and Walt Whitman and Emerson; all was subordinate
to contributing to the general welfare. That's what
she believed in, it seems to me.
Thank you, Ma, complicatedly.

DRAWN

I'd always been drawn
to misunderstandings, almost
as an aesthetic, something
I myself didn't quite fully
misunderstand until now, when
looking back I can see it clearly.

Misunderstanding
after misunderstanding
both external and in-
—It's exhilarating, funny
and the swirls and eddies
rival "Starry Night"

Or Klimt. Oh, dear God
thank you for being
something other
than what you are is
all I can say, and I don't
mean maybe.

PAST IS PAST

Is Kafka about being polite
and ignoring how everything
takes place in an oppressive
cyclical eternity? That
and laughs. Civilization
and its discontents.
I know as much
about such intellectual/historical
matters as the poet (me, for
instance) who doesn't
know the names of flowers
knows flowers, but still I plow
on, trusting
that something worthy
will ensue.
         As it happens
I made a mental note upon encountering
that word ("ensue") the other day
to remember that some form
of it could be used in place
of my habitual subsequent.
Worthiness subsequent to plowing
on. Kafka and
Freud. Einstein, Groucho, Bob
Dylan and Susan Sontag. Mark Rothko.
In old age
I've come to recognize, impolitely
the often especially high intellectual
and empathetic capacities of Jews.

Not that it's done them (us)
a lot of good, broadly. And I've found
myself loving Jewish names that once
had seemed ugly and embarrassing
(though as a child I wasn't aware
of their ethnic import)
just because I grew up
where the names were viewed that way, even
by Jews themselves (in *Mad* magazine
for instance). Now it's different.
Finkelstein sounds noble. I salute
that various field.

oooooooooooooo

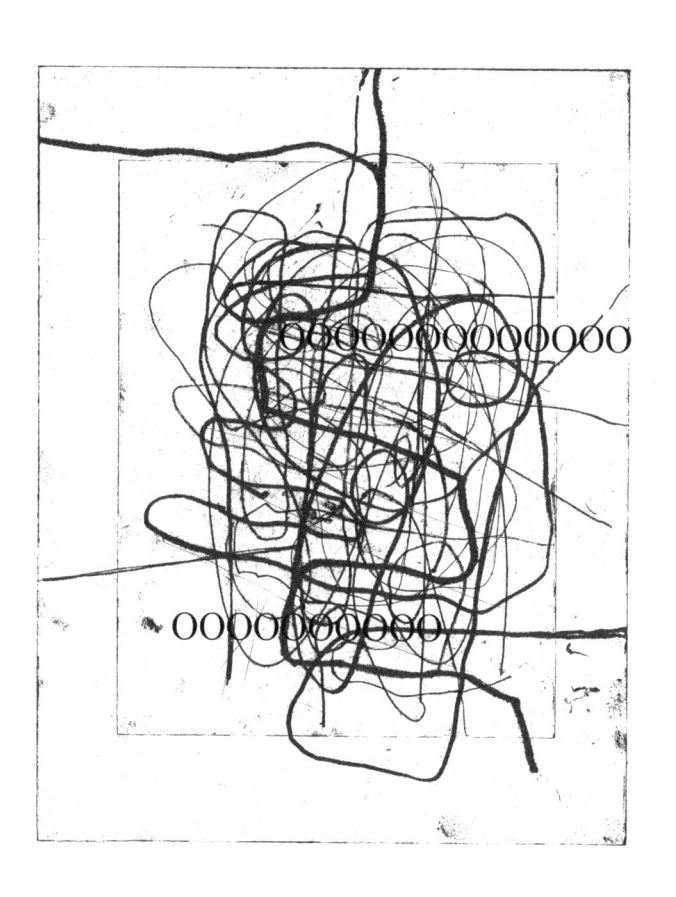

ooooooooo

REFLECTION

A man lounging in an ancient
bathtub perched like a curved porcelain
stock tank on a scaffold of pipe
across from the stove in the kitchen
of his tenement apartment on East 12th Street
New York City, yesterday, July 13th
2021, sitting up to better see
the water slam noisily
into the 18-inch deep pool below
its tarnished brass turn-
handles and spigot
while under that the bubbly
rushing influx plunges
to gently caress his feet, is transfixed.

MY APARTMENT

My apartment is precise
by which I mean
that everything
in it stems
from my preferences—
the books most completely,
but also the chairs,
doorways, tools, carpet,
bureau, closets (armoires),
pictures, couch, table,
windows, desks, and
I could go on—but my
point is that I derive great
satisfaction from
the arrangement, except
when it seems cruelly empty
and all of it coldly
disregards and detaches itself from me.

UNABLE

Unable to travel, or even leave the apartment
much, I wonder how close I can come
to travelling in my mind. There's the famous
passage in *Á rebours*
where Des Esseintes decides against
visiting London because he realizes he's
already gone there in contemplating
it. That made me happy when I found it:
nature as a vulgar form of imagination.
Ennui, a subset of laziness
is largely the fear of being
disturbed (I ought to know).
But here, let me try
to go to London.
For some reason I'm seated uncomfortably
amidst the rustic wood
of this weird private club
someone once took me to.
OK, I'm in the British Museum.
But something's missing.
Or in that kind rock
photographer's humbling bed, which
could happen anywhere. I could
definitely imagine the airplane
ride, but London itself: if only.
Nature is the mind that has
imagined oneself.
Still, there are a lot of surprise
mental destinations too.

This poem is as specific as words'
definitions, and lines' syntax and
enjambment and much more
but look away and it's lost
except for whatever slight alteration
to one's unconscious may've ensued.
Here I am, where the books
dominate like cabinets of views
on walls surrounding me
and in piles, there is no overhead light.
How else could everything in this
room be represented?
Maybe by its shadows?
Sometimes I feel like the Ancient
Mariner, as Coleridge
must have, at least
a little, buttonholing
people with my woes and sins, but
they dominate me as the books
do the room, at least for now.
Why are shadows
associated with wrong
and pain and failure? It's not that hard
to think of reasons, but those
same reasons could underlie poetry.
I'm told Plato thought that everything we see
is shadows—reality removed a dimension or two—
and he wanted to outlaw poetry, but
the shadow idea itself is poetry.

BILL KNOTT READING

I heard a recording of Bill Knott
reading his poems, and the correct
word would be "declaiming"
which surprised me.
I wonder what the roots
of the word "declaim" are.
"Shout thoroughly,"
more or less, and he was, as
if he were an orator.
It worked
though it was unlike how
I myself would have read
aloud his poems, which
are like caves. I
infer that he had a distance
from his own writing.
When he claimed
in an interview that the "I"
in his poems didn't mean him,
he meant it.
I've seen Ted Berrigan
say the same thing, and it's
commonly observed
about Walt Whitman. As might
also be gathered from Rimbaud's
"I is another," receptivity
undoes identity—that's why
they call it the universe (there is
no other, or all there is

is that other)—but each's
poems still embody the given
writer's soul
mystery and so
one's gladdened by it.

CONSOLATION

There's consolation in beauty
but what is beauty?
Not human appearance for instance
which appeals biologically, in signs
of youth and health, and one's further
psychology. Beauty
recalls the incomprehensible
quantity of what happens at once. But
nothing happens "at once" since time
is different at every point in space.
A human life, "circumscribed by the precarious
wonder of its brief apparition," can have no
redemption or salvation.
Therefore so is beauty circumscribed
but for a secret passageway
when your feet branch.

MUMBLES

a chance change of glance
                                         in the glass
            like a snake or cartoonish
       ink depiction of diamonds
                         in the grass—carrots, root
        vegetable, which have, as does all
                a complex backstory
                      that smile dismissing the universe

Kwd T Z jl, A a OJA 9

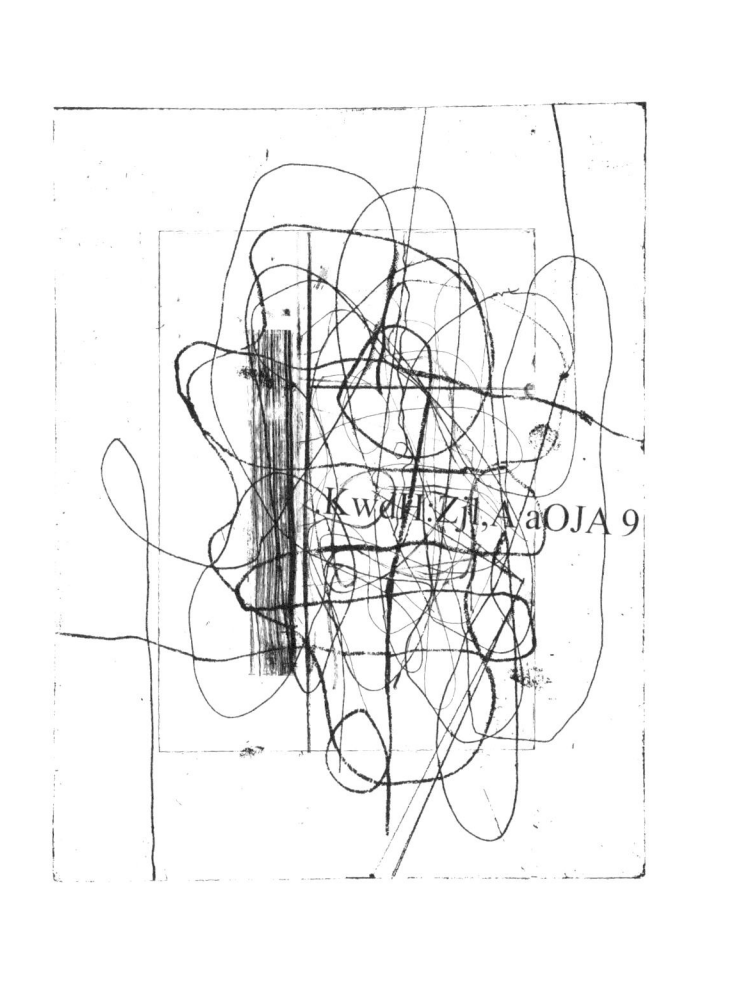

IT'S EASY TO FORGET

It's easy to forget that one has ever done anything, which in a sense is true, one hasn't, and just as well, but it gets frustrating to start from square one over and over. I guess that's the sense in which life is eternal though.

ANNUNCIATION

The original assumption
was that we are the universe looking
at itself, but the more
we looked the less we could see
until it became clear
that we are infinites
imal or, rather, deformed
or rather, that as
observations chained we con
fused with them until
nothing remained but the
original point of departure
or annunciation, which
I always thought meant
being raised to heaven
or being sucked upwards
as if by a vacuum
I don't know
why—not that it's an announcement.
But I prefer my meaning which
I came to honestly and
I feel it
so there's something
in the word or my history
with it that bent it that way.
I received annunciation. It's
my favorite subject for old-
master paintings.
I like the various ways the painters choose

to paint the angel's wings.
I like the presence of the book
that Mary's reading
and the juxtaposition of
interior and ex-.
I knew
it took place in the context
of religion and that it had
to do with something that changed
everything. No, wait, the
original assumption
was that we are
chained in interlocking
causes and effects induced
by god knows what
but apparently both
beautiful and horrifying
in that it seemed self-consistent
somehow though
it encompassed everything
from how a thrown thing
behaves to why there was
a need for the word love
but also inev
itably included dying
which is beneficially
confusing as true.
Oh! That's what—it
was "Assumption"
I confused with
annunciation.

UNTITLED

I miss Sabel Starr and Elliot Kidd
and Bob Quine and Johnny Thunders,
Anya Phillips; imagine
a party with them, we're all sitting around—
like those paintings that '70s Scandinavian
guy used to do of glamorous young
dead artists hanging out in a diner.
I recently acquired a black and white photo
of the interior of CBGB at 4:00 AM closing
time, 1977. Everyone was gone except
for Merv (the manager) and possibly Karen
or a couple of waitresses
or bartenders in the distance tabulating.
It was just litter and bright overhead lights.
I love that picture because it restores
something of myself to me I wouldn't
have otherwise. Now
it's pandemic time. A lot of people must
be looking back. Bill Knott is dead. Denis
Johnson too (he was born
the same year as me—Knott
was some years older). I didn't
know them but I encountered them
both. I never thought a person's
era was all that significant to consider
about them, but it is. There are things
only the people who were together
young, in the time, can understand. And
who else is there to laugh about it

with? No one. Maybe
it's just as well—we do tend to kind
of get twisted with age.
Half of us would have problems with
most of the others. Did at the time.
It's all a mess. It's
crazy my feelings now, lockdown
has released them: I can't get enough
from anyone—all the people I know.
A mess
as I said. These are things that no one
should know, but that's part of poetry, for
better or worse. In my solitude
I'm stripped bare, but now
you're here too, to some degree.

ASSERTION

Why do I want
to make a mark?
I know
better; I know I'll
completely die and so
will the marks
but something wants
to beat death
to the remarkable.

THE THING

The thing about books
on their shelves is how
they look so uniformly
discreet while within is the
meat of all being
human like hues of glittery
or elemental sculpted pouring
into cups of teeny symbols almost
as prettily as the reciprocating
sexual object of one's desires
though mental
usually. On the shelves, each
book separated by its binding
no more combines with another
than anything bound will with
another bound thing but
they do with a person.
The most interesting
thing about minds is
the books that bind them.

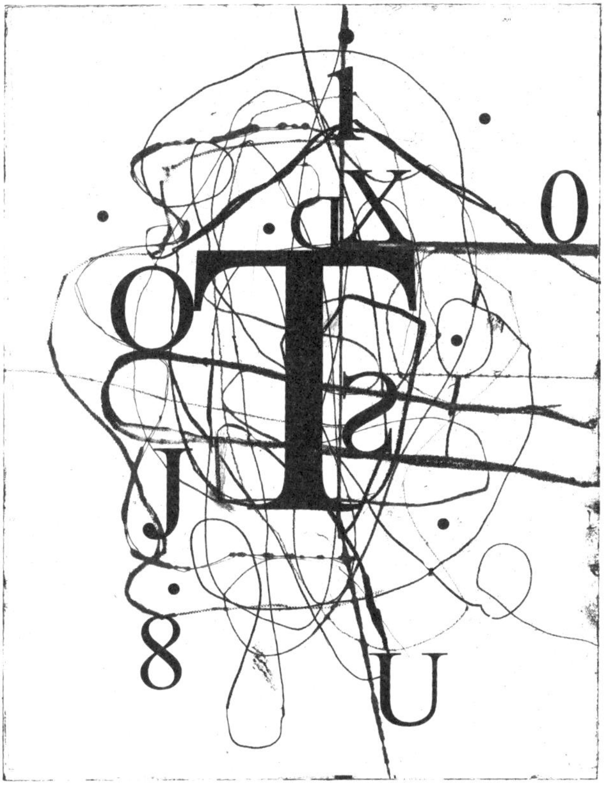

COMPLETE FRAGMENTS

1.

When I observe a pomegranate
in my head, it fills up my entire skull
and I especially notice its ribs, like
the underlying bent wood of a boat's
hull, and also the way the deep
maroon is finely mottled by near
black brownishness and I
remember that the reason a
pomegranate occurs to me
is that yesterday I
read in a footnote on a page of
James Schuyler's *Diary* that Fairfield
Porter's painting called something
like "Interior with a Fabric Pattern"
was partly inspired by a 17th century (?)
Dutch painter's ("De Groot"?) interior called
something like "Boy Delivering a Basket of
Pomegranates."

2.

The Porter is called "Interior with a Dress Pattern" and the 17th century (yes) Dutch painting is by Pieter de Hooch and is called "A Boy Bringing Pomegranates." De Kooning was Dutch. He and Porter were friends and mutual admirers, maybe surprisingly considering how much their painting styles differed. John Ashbery wrote about the particular Porter painting too, in an article (1983) in which he asserted that Porter was "perhaps the major American artist of this century." The two of them were also friends and admirers of each other, though their styles would at first seem way dissimilar. Their underlying intellectual and personal values apparently meant more than what one might guess the styles of their art suggest about the artists' inner beings.

ADVANCED AGE

Advanced age means a decline of faculties.
Sure, much worthwhile can still be done
but there's a natural tendency to focus
on organizing and tying
up old loose ends, and to
re-assess one's past behavior
in light of knowing there's scarce, if any
chance left that it'll improve.
I never before tended much
to dwell on my past. It's awful
to realize that one can no longer assume
the bad behavior was aberrant.
I'm not the person I thought I was.

IDIOSYNCRASY

Familiarity incurs blindness (habit
is the enemy, as per Proust), which is part
of the reason age is dull. Tough people
put a good face on the various ways
one's faculties decline
but the facts remain
stubborn like a skull, memento mori. No
amount of grumbling will alter them either. So
can one learn to enjoy it? I've
thought so when I'm writing well.
In a way, it's merciful, the decline
because it makes dying
more plainly the relief it is.
After all, it can be felt sweetly
as subsidence, as into sleep
or regressing infancy. The dead
and alive are not so dissimilar
so why not embrace that
like a previously worrisome idiosyncrasy?

IT'S THE OBLIVION

It's the oblivion that piques
one's curiosity. Everyone who
has ever lived seems more
the point than any one constituent
but a person has to do
something with the days
just as a bird does. It's odd
and interesting the range
of subjects, of experience
that occupies poets. Anything
goes, in circles
perpetually night outside, though
not in, or there'd be no word night.

POEM

I always feel like what
I write is actually only two thirds
of itself because the other part
is the writing's position
in a story. I mean the poem
is part of something else
that determines
and completes it, and
that other thing is indescribable. Say
you are reading this now, which
is a pretty safe bet, but
no; in fact, I am writing it.

CONTINUATION

As I was waking up, wondering whether to get out of bed, I realized I couldn't remember the name of my dog, and I thought, That's it, dementia for sure, and then I remembered that I've never had a dog.

·

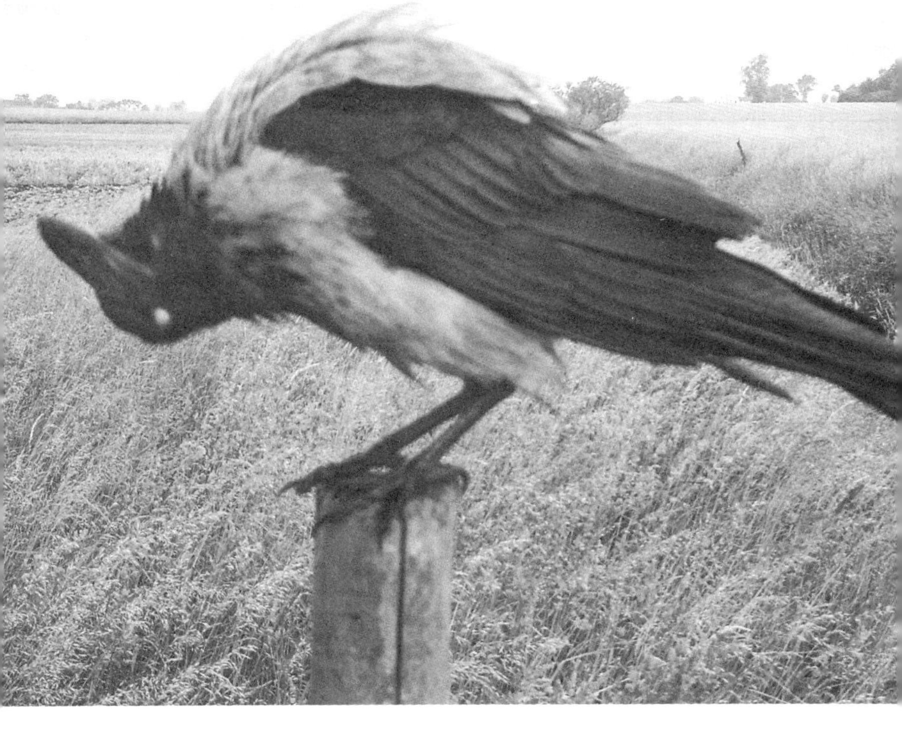

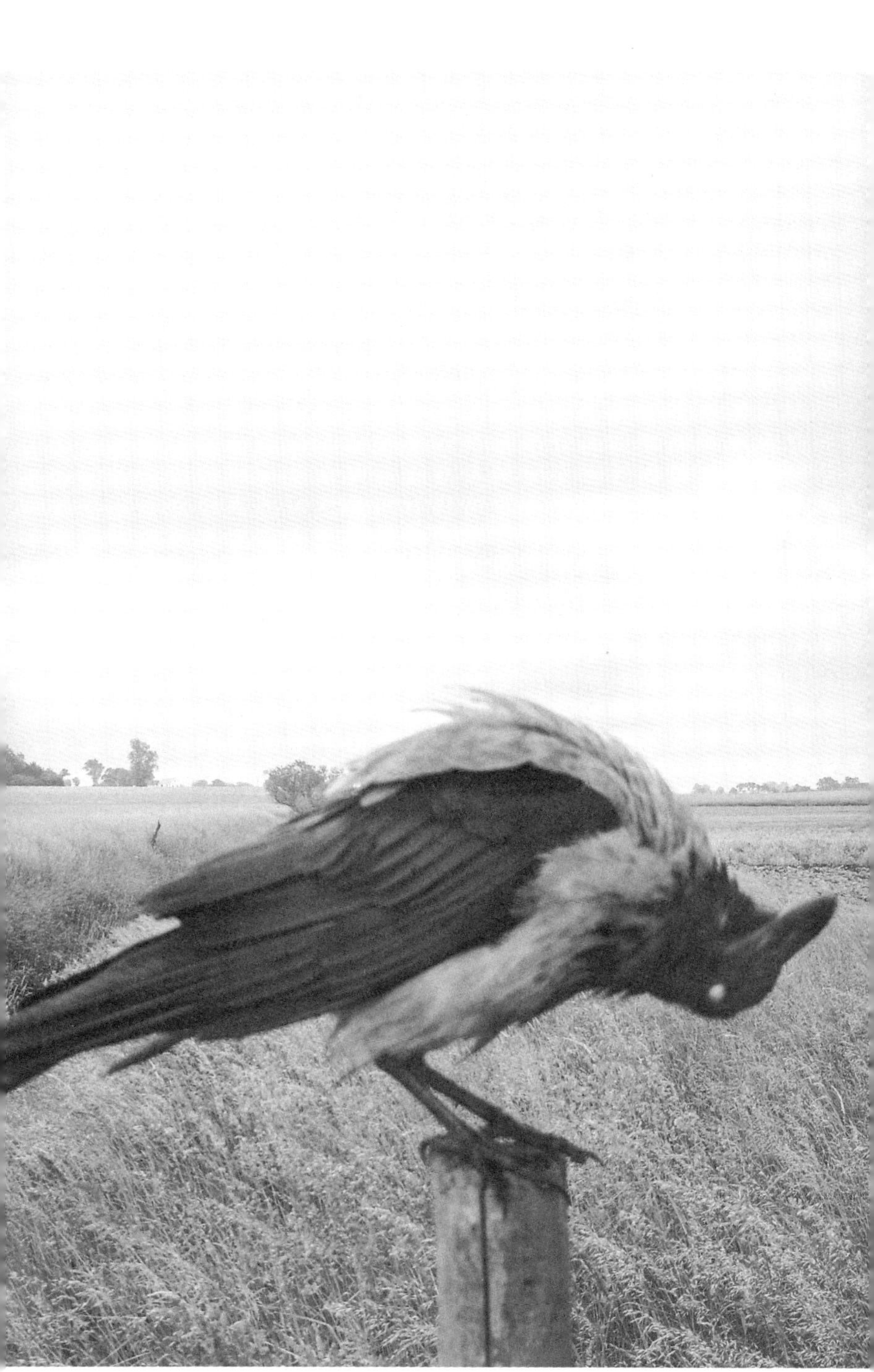

What Just Happened

essay & list

FALLING ASLEEP

I dropped out of high school to be a poet, so I needed to try to teach myself, by reading and writing, how to write. My first big insight was that poetry is metaphor (is that a metaphor?), in metaphor's broadest sense—the evocation of something by invoking something else. Life is a dream, or death as sleep, and "even your shoulders are petty crimes" or "the hum-colored cabs." Do those last two count as metaphors? I don't know. Maybe the shoulders were committed in innocence. But ignorance of the law excuses not. What if all metaphors are literal? Inside a dog it's too dark to read.

Language is about something meaning something else, just as it's about a thing only existing in relationship to other things. As Borges pointed out in his late talk "The Metaphor," [*This Craft of Verse,* Harvard, 2000] it's been said—in the instance by Lugones—that words themselves are metaphors, in the sense that they contain other, underlying, prior meanings that have come to have the overriding meaning of the present word. An example Borges gives is "king" which derives from "cyning," an Old English word that originally meant "a man who stands for the kin—for the people." So, maybe the king is no longer related to all his subjects, but metaphorically he is, because of his title. And, to get even more abstract, words are metaphors in that they themselves, a sequence of alphabet letters or of sounds indicate the objects, acts and relationships, etc., they convey. Or is that wrong because the resemblance is arbitrary? (Yes it is.) There's nothing about the sequence s, t, o, n, e, or the sound it signals, in themselves, that has anything in common with a stone. (Then again, humming hums.) Except that...? (And words start seeming similar to that to which they refer.) And to pull back from the word to entire poems, the poems of many recent writers—John Ashbery, for instance— while not much operating in the classical way of using metaphor to refresh our sensation or understanding of phenomena, seem to be themselves metaphors for the poet's inner being,[1] or the tenor of it at the time of composition. "Tenor" in the context of the concept of metaphor means the subject in the metaphor, while "vehicle" denotes how that subject is getting re-imaginatively evoked. For instance, Roy Orbison hummed like chauffered teal.

The longer I live, the more I can see patterns in my experiences and behavior and everyone else's. That's logical. A number of those accumulated, ever-provisional deductions seem to be converging now, drawn together by their density into an ultimate: that reality most resembles wherein combine wakefulness and sleep, the living and the inanimate. This is not unknown; another thing a person learns is that nothing's original.

Existence takes place outside of life and non-life, but at their intersection or the space between them, or their combination, and one way or another art is about this situation and is rooted in it. Reality is the mixture of consciousness (self-aware life) and the unconscious/inanimate (I'm trying to include everything) and art is how humans investigate and express that territory.

---

[1] That inner being is a dream. All is a dream. Life is a dream. Death's dream. We are the dream of the dead, the inanimate. We arose from the dead universe: heat and light and water and rock. We are its dream, the dream of mud, and when we fall asleep we come nearest to what things are.

> Humans brainwash you. But humans and families and jobs aren't the world. We're just another feeling of the world. We're just dirt that talks. Our job is to speak for the dirt. Stand up for the mud.
> —from "Huck Hell & Legs Sawyer on the Mississippi" (with Legs McNeil, *Spin* magazine, 1986)

> The stranger has a cigar and is observing geese
> pass across the moon like an intricate model ship
> or symphonic violins, and all I can do is dream of
>   mud, oh mud, mud.
> —Theresa Stern, from "You Stranger I'm Tight and Juicy" (with Tom Verlaine, *Wanna Go Out*, Dot Books, 1973)

> I have this theory about mud, too. People say we're made of stars. "Star stuff." That's alright, but who knows about the stars? I say we're made of mud. Watery mud. If you could see it all at once you'd see mud getting up and talking. And then you're right when we go to sleep we're mud again. Maybe we're the dream of mud...
> —from *The Theresa Stern Story* (unpublished film script, 1988)

In terms of direct human experience, reality most resembles the area between wakefulness and sleep, and "Between Wakefullness and Sleep" was the name of an essay published by Edgar Allen Poe in 1846.

> There is, however, a class of fancies, of exquisite delicacy, which are not thoughts, and to which, as yet, I have found it absolutely impossible to adapt language. I use the word fancies at random, and merely because I must use some word; but the idea commonly attached to

the term is not even remotely applicable to the shadows of shadows in question. They seem to me rather psychal than intellectual. They arise in the soul (alas, how rarely!) only at its epochs of most intense tranquility—when the bodily and mental health are in perfection—and at those mere points of time where the confines of the waking world blend with those of the world of dreams. I am aware of these "fancies" only when I am upon the very brink of sleep, with the consciousness that I am so. I have satisfied myself that this condition exists but for an inappreciable point of time yet it is crowded with these "shadows of shadows"; and for absolute thought there is demanded time's endurance.

These "fancies" have in them a pleasurable ecstasy, as far beyond the most pleasurable of the world of wakefulness, or of dreams, as the Heaven of the Northman theology is beyond its Hell. I regard the visions, even as they arise, with an awe which, in some measure moderates or tranquillises the ecstasy—I so regard them, through a conviction (which seems a portion of the ecstasy itself) that this ecstasy, in itself, is of a character supernal to the Human Nature—is a glimpse of the spirit's outer world; and I arrive at this conclusion—if this term is at all applicable to instantaneous intuition—by a perception that the delight experienced has, as its element, but the absoluteness of novelty. I say the absoluteness—for in the fancies—let me now term them psychal impressions—there is really nothing even approximate in character to impressions ordinarily received. It is as if the five senses were supplanted by five myriad others alien to mortality.
—Edgar Allen Poe, from "Between Wakefulness and Sleep" (1846) in *The Unknown Poe*, ed. Raymond Foye (City Lights, 2001)

HAND SHADOWS

> When all the yellow birds came flying
> into my fingers, I thought they were
> roses someone didn't want, the kind
> of gift an audience gives to its
> favorite violinist. But I'm not
> a violinist and they were not roses.
> They were birds.
> —Jamie MacInnis, from *Practicing* (Tombouctou, 1974)

Which leads to another hypothesis: that in the last two hundred or so years, the half-asleep condition, wherein one dreams but has some consciousness of the experience—what's been termed "hypnagogia"—has become the ground of much art and thought, Freud and surrealism being probably the most obvious examples, but also reaching back to Nerval and Poe and Redon and Rimbaud ("All known literature is written in the language of common sense—except Rimbaud's." —Paul Valéry, 1899) and forward to Pollock and Ashbery.

> Our dreams are a second life. I have never been able to penetrate without a shudder those ivory or horned gates which separate us from the invisible world. The first moments of sleep are an image of death; a hazy torpor grips our thoughts and it becomes impossible for us to determine the exact instant when the "I," under another form, continues the task of existence. Little by little a vague underground cavern grows lighter and the pale gravely immobile shapes that live in limbo detach themselves from the shadows and the night. Then the

picture takes form, a new brightness illumines these strange apparitions and gives them movement. The spirit world opens before us.

—Gérard de Nerval, from *Aurélia* (1855), *Aurélia & Other Writings* (Exact Change, 2004), trans. Geoffrey Wagner

THEY DREAM ONLY OF AMERICA

They dream only of America
To be lost among the thirteen million pillars of grass:
"This honey is delicious
Though it burns the throat."

And hiding from darkness in barns
They can be grownups now
And the murderer's ash tray is more easily—
The lake a lilac cube.

He holds a key in his right hand.
"Please," he asked willingly.
He is thirty years old.
That was before

We could drive hundreds of miles
At night through dandelions.
When his headache grew worse we
Stopped at a wire filling station.

Now he cared only about signs.
Was the cigar a sign?
And what about the key?
He went slowly into the bedroom.

"I would not have broken my leg if I had not fallen
Against the living room table. What is it to be back
Beside the bed? There is nothing to do
For our liberation, except wait in the horror of it."

And I am lost without you.
—John Ashbery, from *The Tennis Court Oath* (Wesleyan
University Press, 1962)

[A]rt is human willpower deploying every means at its disposal to break through to a truer state than the present one."
—John Ashbery, from "Writers and Issues: Frank O'Hara" (1966) in *Selected Prose* (University of Michigan Press, 2004)

A further, and recent, as well as the most speculative and tenuous of this convergence of intimations I've been experiencing, is that perhaps our long hallucinatory era's preoccupation with this hynagogic state is a sign of the end times. As sleep is like death, our recent centuries' incorporation of sleep into "rationality," into wakefulness, is a further sign (along with such things as weapons of mass destruction and apocalyptic climate change) that humanity is reaching its end.

Nobody knows what sleep is.

In another story, the mind-haunting "Human Moments in World War III," Vollmer, an astronaut in his twenties, gazes down on Earth as he and the narrator collect imagery data on troop deployment. Radio signals from decades earlier somehow infect their transmissions from mission control. "A quality of purest, sweetest sadness issued from remote space." As they work to control the "lethal package" they are dealing with, they look at Earth and fall into reverie: "The cities are in light, the listening millions, fed, met comfortably in drowsy rooms, at war, as the night comes softly down." The story feels like an elegy to the planet and takes its place in the growing literature of preapocalyptic writing, intensified in this particular case by the narrator's distance (he's in orbit) and his sense that he and Vollmer are observing a planetary body that is about to disappear altogether with their willing cooperation. The grief over the fate of Earth infuses into the story a tone of immense melancholy. [...]

One thinks of the lines from Beckett's *Molloy*: "From things about to disappear I turn away in time. To watch them out of sight, no, I can't do it." However, Vollmer has not yet turned away, not quite. He's still watching, still looking, still occupying that passing moment of contemplation before the object of his gaze—the thing about to disappear—is gone.

And here we arrive at the necessary component of the trance experience, the implicit content at its core: the narcotic spectacle of an entity's fragile existence prior to its violent death or destruction. The prospect of an imminent violent death renders everyone speechless and thoughtful. It is the pre-apocalyptic condition. In this fiction, violent death occupies a privileged position in the hierarchy of signifiers. The thing about to be destroyed takes on a terrible beauty, worthy of elegy.

—from Charles Baxter's review of Don DeLillo's *The Angel Esmeralda: Nine Stories*, in the *New York Review of Books* (February 9, 2012)

I've always had a hard time remaining in the particulars of experience. I more want to know the connections between them or the reasons behind them or their implications. This is part of the reason I didn't turn out to be a poet. I want to think and reach conclusions about how things are on an abstract or divine level—"how things are" is my understanding of God—rather than remain in local experience. I want more. I want everything. I want to be God. I don't regard this as being positive or negative, except when I do. It's temperament. Another insight in trying to figure out how to write a good poem was that it's the poet's duty not to understand, because we don't and can't, and to pretend otherwise is to eliminate poetry. The part of the mind that understands excludes it. We don't know anything. Poetry is revery, not understanding, because reality is revery.

> [A]t once it struck me what quality went to form a Man of Achievement, especially in Literature, and which Shakespeare possessed so enormously—I mean Negative Capability, that is, when a man is capable of being in uncertainties, mysteries, doubts, without any irritable reaching after fact and reason [...]
> —John Keats, letter to his brothers George and Thomas, December 1817 [These days people use F. S. Fitzgerald's variation more often. He said, in *The Crack-Up* (New Directions, 1945), that "the test of a first-rate intelligence is the ability to hold two opposed ideas in the mind at the same time, and still retain the ability to function."]

It's as if consciousness itself is the entity, by definition our universe, and the consciousness of each particular human is only a portion of it, an aspect. "Understanding" takes place in individual consciousness, which is always vastly incomplete, and everything individual is reflexive. It's as if consciousness were a sphere, the surface of which is made of points or tiny polygons each of which is one of all the existing humans—to restrict ourselves to the only conscious beings of which we're aware—facing inward towards the universe, each having only the limited access to the whole available from that particular point, just as each can only be affected by its particular experience, while at the same time we are nearly identical as the composition of the sphere of consciousness itself, and are linked, like the neurons in the brain.

One's inner being is a dream. All is a dream. Life is a dream. This is not to trivialize it: there is pain and "injustice" and matters of great human importance in dreams too; it's just that we regard dreams as unreal: no, dreams are where we're exposed most directly to reality, the bending of things through us, the junction of us and what is.

What we perceive via our eyes, nose, ears, touch, tongue for instance, is not "real." It is created by our brains. What we deem light/color, odors and sounds are a few of the sorts of particles/waves permeating the universe, most of which we don't perceive at all (less than 1% of the entire spectrum of light is visible to the unaided human eye), but some of which, locally useful, are turned into qualities by our brains, turned into signaling meta-correspondences called the likes of chartreuse and musk and a piano middle C (and wet and salty). But how we perceive the wave-lengths of photons, for instance, has nothing to do with what they "actually" are, except that the structure of the relationships between the various wavelengths corresponds to the structure of the relationships among the sensations we describe as "colors." There is nothing otherwise meaningful about either the limited categories of data in the universe our senses have access to or about the particular forms that data is translated into for our purposes. They're dreams, like mythemes through which we swim; they're a forest of symbols, synesthetically blending too, in literal metaphors, as we dream them and are dreamt by them, as Baudelaire wrote.

CORRESPONDENCES

Nature is a temple whose columns are alive and sometimes issue disjointed messages. We thread our way through a forest of symbols that peer out, as if recognizing us.

Like long echoes from far away, merging into a deep dark unity, vast as night, vast as the light, smells and colors and sounds concur.

There are perfumes cool as children's flesh, sweet as oboes, green like the prairie. And others corrupt, rich, overbearing,

with the expansiveness of infinite things — like ambergris, musk, spikenard, frankincense, singing ecstasy to the mind and to the senses.

—Charles Baudelaire, from *Les Fleurs du Mal* (1857) as published in *Flowers of Evil* (Wesleyan University Press, 2006), trans. Keith Waldrop [It's a sonnet rendered as prose quatrain/tercet "versets" in stanzaic divisions.]

Then, within, we have no way of understanding anything except for how it operates in relation to other things. Not only words themselves, but the things that the words refer to are only known by their relationships to other such things. A stone is smaller than a boulder, bigger than a pebble, probably. Also hard and dense, not soft or liquid (though volcanic stone is like stiffened foam). And the thing called a stone is the way it behaves in relation to other behaviors. Without something to contrast it to, there is no stone. It only exists mentally, and as a relationship to other mental constructs.

> Dreams were another of the facts of my life which had always most profoundly impressed me and had done most to convince me of the purely mental character of reality [...]
> —Marcel Proust, *Time Regained* (1927), (Modern Library Classics, 1999), trans. Andreas Mayor and Terence Kilmartin, revised by D.J. Enright and Joanna Kilmartin

Proust initiates his 3000 page novel with an evocation of the state of falling asleep ("[...]my eyes would close so quickly that I had not even time to say to myself: 'I'm falling asleep.' And half an hour later the thought that it was time to go to sleep would awaken me; I would make as if to put away the book which I imagined was still in my hands, and to blow out the light; I had gone on thinking, while I was asleep, about what I had just been reading, but these thoughts had taken a rather peculiar turn; it seemed to me that I myself was the immediate subject of my book [...]")

The writer who most reminds me of Proust is the anthropologist Claude Lévi-Strauss. His account of his stay among tribes in the Amazonian jungle, *Tristes Tropiques*, is as perceptive, frank, intelligent, personal, and literarily sophisticated as *In Search of Lost Time*, and the prose styles of the two can resemble each other. Most of Lévi-Strauss's other writings are anthropological treatises less accessible to laypeople. His thinking, as evidenced in *Triste Tropiques*, was affected by Saussure's ideas about linguistics, referred to by Lévi-Strauss as structuralism. Lévi-Strauss believed that Saussure's theory or insight that the underlying structure of human languages was universal also applied to other systems of cultural expression than linguistics, such as mythology or tribal mask-making. A finding of his studies was that the universal function of myths was to reconcile opposite or conflicting realities for the given culture: man and woman, war and peace, plant and animal—almost any significant duality—while the ultimate, the foundational opposition to be bridged, perhaps, was that of nature and culture (unconscious nature and conscious human beings).

> We imagine infirmity and sickness to be deprivations of being and therefore evil. However, if death is as real as life, and if therefore everything is being, all states, even pathological ones, are positive in their own way. 'Negativized being' is entitled to occupy a whole place within the system, since it is the only conceivable means of a transition between two 'full' states."
> —Claude Lévi-Strauss, *The Raw and the Cooked* (1964) (Harper and Row, 1969)

Death is as real as life and therefore everything is being. A screwy thing about the whole discussion of the juncture of life and death, is that in another sense it's the material cosmos which is immortal, while we, supposedly alive, die.

GOLDEN LINES

> "And so! Everything is alive!"
> —*Pythagoras*

Man, free thinker! Do you believe you alone can think
In this world where life bursts forth in everything?
Your freedom disposes what it may
But the universe is beyond you.

In animals honor the mind acting:
Each flower is a soul disclosed by Nature;
A mystery of love lies concealed in metal;
"Everything is alive!" and has power over you.

Beware in the blind wall a gaze that watches you:
The heart of matter holds a word ...
Make it serve no impious use!

Often in the obscure being hides a God;
And like the eye born under the eyelid's veil,
Pure spirit grows beneath the skin of stones.
—Gérard de Nerval, from *Les Chimeres* (1854), trans. Richard Hell

I was saying let me out of here before I was even born.
It's such a gamble when you get a face.
It's fascinating to observe what the mirror does
but when I dine it's for the wall that I set a place.
—from "Blank Generation" (1974)

The poet Octavio Paz understood, in the context of his reading of Lévi-Strauss—specifically the anthropologist's initial full-scale study of Amazonian native mythology, *The Raw and the Cooked*—that death was the reality that underlay all manifestations of culture. It is knowing that we must die that makes us human, is the definition of consciousness, thereby the source of culture.

> The real theme of all these myths is the opposition between culture and nature as it is expressed in the human creation *par excellence*: the cooking of foods over a domestic fire. A Promethean theme with many echoes: the schism between the gods and men, the eternal life of the cosmos and the brief life of human beings, but likewise the mediation between life and death, sky and water, plants and animals. It would be useless to try to list all the ramifications of this opposition since it encompasses every aspect of human life. It is a theme which leads us to the center of Lévi-Strauss's meditation: the place of man in nature. The position of cooking as an activity which at once separates and unites the natural world and the human world is [...] prefigured by language which is what separates us from nature and what unites us to it and to our fellow men. Language signifies the distance between man and things as well as the will to erase it. Cooking [...] is a mediation between the raw and decayed, the animal world and the vegetable [...]. [Its] model [...] is the word, the bridge between the shout and silence, between the nonsignificance of nature and the insignificance of men. [...] [Both] are screens which filter the anonymous natural world and turn it into names, signs, and qualities. They change

the shapeless torrent of life into a discrete quantity and into families of symbols. In [...] [both], the texture of the screen is made up of an intangible substance: death. Lévi-Strauss hardly mentions it. Perhaps his proud materialism keeps him from mentioning it. In addition, from a certain point of view, death is only another manifestation of immortal living matter. But how can we fail to see in that need to distinguish between nature and culture, in order to introduce a mediating term between the two of them, the echo and the obsession of knowing ourselves to be mortal?

Death is the real difference, the dividing line between man and the current of life. The ultimate meaning of all those metaphors is death. Cooking [...] and language are operations of the spirit, but the spirit is an operation of death. Although the need to survive through nourishment [...] is common to all living things, the wiles with which man confronts this inevitability make him a different being. To feel oneself and know oneself to be mortal is to be different: death condemns us to culture. Without it there would be no arts or trades: language, cooking, and kinship rules are mediations between the immortal life of nature and the brevity of human existence. Here Lévi-Strauss agrees with Freud and, at the other extreme, with Hegel and Marx. Closer to the latter two than the former, in a second movement his thought tries to dissolve the dichotomy between culture and nature—not by means of work, history, or revolution, but by knowledge of the laws of the human spirit. The mediator between brief life and natural immortality is the spirit: an unconscious and collective device, as immortal and anonymous as a cell. [...] [I]t is by its origin on the side of nature, and by its function and its products on the side of culture. In the opposition between death and life, the discrete significance of man and the infinite nonsignificance of the cosmos is almost erased. Facing death the spirit is life, and facing the latter, death. From the beginning, human understanding has been completely unable—because it is logically impossible—to explain nothingness by being or being by nothingness. Perhaps the spirit is the mediator. In the area of physics, we reach similar conclusions: Professor John Wheeler, at a recent meeting of the Physical Society, asserted that it is impossible to locate an event in time or space: before and after, here and there, are abstracts without meaning. There is a point at which "something is nothing and nothing is something."

—Octavio Paz, *Claude Lévi-Strauss: An Introduction* (Cornell, 1970)

One could have the viewpoint that, as dreams can reveal otherwise unconscious conflicts and thereby enable some resolutions for the individual dreamer, myths attempt to reconcile conflicts or mysteries for a culture. Myths feel like dreams that explain how things became as they are, and what one's position is in this reality, thereby easing the anxiety, as this essay eases my trepidations about suffering death (now that I'm old). The only system of mythology, apart from monotheistic religions, that most of the industrialized west knows to any meaningful extent is the ancient Greek and Roman. I'll stick to the Greek, since it was the original.

Hypnos was a primordial deity in Greek mythology, the personification of sleep. He lived in a cave next to his twin brother, Thanatos [death—though sometimes specified as peaceful death in contrast to the Keres, who embodied violent death] in the underworld, where no light was cast by the sun or the moon; the earth in front of the cave was full of poppies and other sleep-inducing plants. The river Lethe (the river of forgetfulness) flowed through the cave. Hypnos was the son of Nyx (night), in some acounts without a father, but in others fathered by Erebus (darkness) [both Nyx and Erebus being among the original five divine beings, offspring of primordial Chaos], while his wife, Pasithea [relaxation, meditation, and such hallucinatory states of consciousness at rest], was one of the youngest of the Graces and was given to him by Hera [in exchange for Hypnos causing Zeus to sleep, thereby permitting the Greeks to win the Trojan War]. Hypnos and Pasithea had a number of sons called the Oneiroi (the dreams).

—a pastiche of information from Wikipedia

That description is intended to be as accurate as possible, but not only do the available ancient chronicles of mythology vary—just as in tribal Brazil, different ancient Greek precincts believed local versions of their hugely complex living mythology—but it's a primary characteristic of myths that they vary in their retelling, and the variations are valid. The myths are eternal but they are always morphing[2] in the individuality of their manifestation in

---

2 Morpheus, which name derives from the Greek word for "form," and who appears in the Roman Ovid's account of mythological episodes, *Metamorphoses*, is a son of Somnus—the Roman equivalent of Hypnos— and is said to appear in dreams as their human inhabitants, thereby

any person's transmission. Lévi-Strauss called his book of structural myth analysis a myth.[3] (It should be noted that Lévi-Strauss rarely analyzed myths from more layered and complex societies like the Greek/Roman or the Mayan, because of concern that the myths' emphases could have been warped in their transmission to favor certain rulers or gods.)

Incidentally,

> 'Narcissus' (nárkissos) was the ancient-Greek word for the flower, native to southern Europe, that we commonly call the daffodil. The word 'narcissus' is related to the Greek nárke, or torpor, numbness, a narcotic quality; it comes from the myth of Narcissus, the beautiful youth who became entranced by his own reflection."
> —Mary Norris, "Greek to Me" in the *New Yorker*, January 14, 2019

I have been called narcissistic. No I haven't—I've been called solipsistic. But I do like narcotics (though I've learned it's best to avoid them) and they induce precisely the state between wakefulness and sleep that this essay proposes as the closest that consciousness can come to reality. When I was first exposed to a strong narcotic and I tried to analyze what the most seductive quality of it was, I figured it was the way it allowed you to dream while remaining in a conscious enough state (nod) that

---

"mimicking many forms," though he's not mentioned in surviving ancient sources prior to Ovid, and may have been an addition of his to the pantheon, god bless him.

3 "[I]t would not be wrong to consider this book itself as a myth: it is, as it were, the myth of mythology."—*The Raw and the Cooked*, p. 12

you could deliberately influence what would happen next in the dream.

> I do not ask of God that he should change anything in events themselves, but that he should change me in regard to things, so that I might have the power to create my own universe about me, to govern my own dreams instead of enduring them.
> —Gérard de Nerval as quoted by Arthur Symons in *The Symbolist Movement in Literature* (Dutton, 1919)

Now there is another, deeper meaning of dreamtime—which is of a time that is no time, just an enduring state of being. There is an important myth from Indonesia that tells of this mythological age and its termination. In the beginning, according to this story, the ancestors were not distinguished as to sex. There were no births, there were no deaths. Then a great public dance was celebrated, and in the course of the dance one of the participants was trampled to death and torn to pieces, and the pieces were buried. At the moment of that killing the sexes became separated, so that death was balanced by begetting, begetting by death, while from the buried parts of the dismembered body food plants grew. Time had come into being, death, birth, and the killing and eating of other living beings, for the preservation of life. The timeless time of the beginning had terminated by a communal crime, a deliberate murder or sacrifice. Now, one of the problems of mythology is reconciling the mind to this brutal precondition of all life, which lives by the killing and eating of lives. You don't kid yourself by eating only vegetables, either, for they, too,

are alive. So the essence of life is this eating of itself! Life lives on life, and the reconciliation of the human mind and sensibilities to that fundamental fact is one of the functions of some of those very brutal rites in which the ritual consists chiefly of killing— in imitation, as it were, of that first, primordial crime, out of which arose this temporal world, in which we all participate. The reconciliation of mind to the conditions of life is fundamental to all creation stories. They're very like each other in this aspect.
—Joseph Campbell interviewed by Bill Moyers, *The Power of Myth* (Anchor, 1991)

"Now there is another, deeper meaning of dreamtime— which is of a time that is no time, just an enduring state of being."

> I settled into run-of-the-mill hallucinations. I very clearly saw a mosque in place of a factory, a group of drummers consisting of angels, carriages on the heavenly highways, a sitting room at the bottom of a lake; monsters, mysteries, the title of a vaudeville could conjure anything.
> —Arthur Rimbaud, "Delirium II: The Alchemy of Words" *A Season in Hell* (1873) (Modern Library, 2002), trans. Wyatt Mason

It seemed to me that everyone should have had several other lives as well. This gentleman doesn't know what he's doing; he's an angel. That family is a litter of puppy dogs. With some men, I often talked out loud with a

> moment from one of their other lives—that's how I happened to love a pig.
>
> —Arthur Rimbaud, "Delirium II: The Alchemy of Words," *A Season in Hell* (1873) (HarperCollins, 1975), trans. Paul Schmidt

Dreamtime, when one is conscious enough on the outskirts of sleep to retain into consciousness some quantity of dream experience, is ahistorical, just as a given system of mythologies is. The same could be said of all daily life. You don't have to go very deep to reach the network of experiences shared—with varying emphases—by practically all humans throughout time. Working for sustenance, sleeping, eating, having sex, dealing with social interactions, all the common aims and problems. There's a universal structure there too apart from history.

All my life I've loved falling asleep. I suppose most people feel the same except that many don't quite consider sleep to be part of life unless it's forced on their attention somehow and even then it's just a meaningless natural function, like peeing, that's actually peripheral to life. But what is falling asleep? At its most concentrated it's the way one feels after an orgasm or after partaking of an opiate. It's fleshly comfort and mild, carnivalesque delirium. Of course it can startle and threaten and frighten too, but what I'm referring to is hypnagogia at its essence, unhampered by pain or significant conscious turmoil, the components of insomnia.... As Poe pointed out, the experience we're invoking occurs only "upon the very brink of sleep, with the consciousness that [one is] so," and, "when the bodily and mental health are in perfection—and at those mere points of time where the confines of the waking world blend with those of the world of dreams." It can go wrong.

> as gregor samsa awoke one morning from uneasy dreams he found himself transformed in his bed into a gigantic insect he was laying on his hard as if were armor plated back and when he lifted his head a little he could see his domelike brown belly divided into stiff arched segments on top of which the bed quilt could hardly keep in position and was about to slide off completely his numerous legs which were pitifully thin compared to the rest of his bulk waved helplessly before his eyes

—Franz Kafka, "The Metamorphosis" (1915), *Franz Kafka: The Complete Stories* (Schocken, 1976), trans. Willa and Edwin Muir [Punctuation and upper case removed by R. Hell.]

I dream of falling asleep.

That's my dream. How did "dream" as the word for the apparent experiences or visions we have when we're asleep become the word also for a person's hopes and aspirations (foolish or not)? I suppose it's not very complicated, though I see in an etymological dictionary that that particular meaning of "dream" ("It's my dream to be world champion.") is recent, the 1930s (though it's also the case that Diogenes Laertius, in his *Lives and Opinions of Eminent Philosophers* circa the third century AD, quotes Aristotle as defining hope as "a waking dream"). The hint or taint of that meaning of the word lamentably complicates its use though. Except I dream of falling asleep.

The sweetness of the dream of falling asleep is partly erotic.

THAT TO THE SIDES OF THE DARK SHINE THE THEORIES

Yesterday, late in the evening, I started feeling thick and heavy as if I were being pulled down, as if something deep underground had started to exert a new kind of gravity that was sucking my body and senses toward it, while my floating mind stayed above. I could hardly keep my eyelids raised and I had to lie down. Once I did that, my body hollowed and lightened, like a drawing of itself. My mind seemed to float loose while leaking into my body like molecules: sex, sax, six, socks, sucks... It was like my body liquified, then evaporated, then rained, the whole prehistoric breathing, and my mind was a rudderless little boat that drifted in it. I seeped and haltingly flowed according to the permeability and slant. In the puddles at the bottom of the boat was a tumbled messy litter of everything imaginable that had happened or could happen to me. How could it be so small? My senses seemed to have returned, but were caught in the contents of the boat, as if perception were engendered by those objects.[1] It seemed that if I looked at one item—a tan-colored lifesize hobbyshop model of a robin, for instance—everything else in the strew became possible, so that when my attention left the glued-together plastic bird, the items around it had become something other than what they'd been before. Oh, it was too beautiful, this surrender. It is the secret standard of worthiness. All who do it are good! My mind[2] opened and the boat, being one, the only, wasn't a boat.[3]

1 Later I heard "that to the sides of the dark shine the theories."*

2 If the brain-neurons are buzzing, are individual, can choose, aren't they all of life and history? Each person is God and the brain's neurons are all the people of the history of the world. We are the neurons in God's brain. (Is God asleep? Will God awake? And then what happens to us? God's wakefulness the laws, God's sleep the activity...)

3 Somewhere in the ocean I started getting an erection. Marilyn Monroe had a penis. The boat sprang a leak. I "woke up"** with come all over me.

---

* If you want to be an artist, go to sleep.

** Falling, going to, then coming, up...

—from *Hot and Cold* (powerHouse, 2001)

Our intelligence is the capacity for recognizing patterns in our experience and sorting them into cause and effect. For instance I think that the universe is intelligent because it seems logical that intelligence—ours—could only be generated by intelligence. At the same time I know that saying a thing like that has no meaning. It's just my fate to be driven to surmise. I also believe that reality starts where knowledge ends.

The older I get the less there seems to be a world. Things arrive and depart from the apparent. In my experience, the world kept shifting shape until the whole process broke down as did "the world." There's no scale. Everything is equally complex no matter its size. Nothing changes: it all simply modulates incomprehensibly.

Equally, one might say the world is a ridiculous reduction. Look at how things are, given the infinite that's hidden.

It's preoccupied sluggishness, a laziness, an indifference that's excited, excitement that's indifferent. A dreaminess. I wonder about what the connotations of "poet" are, what people mean when they call someone a poet when it's not about writing poems. It's a person who's impractical, who cares about underlying realities more than worldly ambition and appearances, who's absent minded. Drunken. Also good-willed, spiritually generous. Yes? Perhaps mildly provocative. A cloud in pants. It's because it's impractical to metaphor interminably, write poetry, it's like forgetting how to walk: it will not pay the rent. That's one of the beauties of poetry, it's the place of fewest false values. A commitment to beauty as ridiculous as looking at the clouds all day, preferably a curious and therefore analytic commitment. Poets are fools.

> Poets are fools but I don't give a fuck
> anymore. Life's only good when it's well written.
> —from "New Year's Day 2001" (2001), *Disgusting* (38th St. Books, 2010)

The erosion that comes with age of certain mental faculties is like entering a more dreamlike state, as if you're gradually increasing your resemblance to the inanimate, where chance and physics, rather than any illusory will, are clearly the only actors. One can catch one's mind behaving the way dreams develop: when one has just been thinking of something and then momentarily gotten distracted and then can remember what had been on one's mind but it's a mistaken memory that can have been triggered by any quality of the thing or word(s) for the thing one had in mind; for instance, say one had been thinking of a briefcase, the misremembered item could be a briar case or a saddle or a court date or etc. It's the same way dreams develop: a cat could be or become a car or a bat or a dog or a snarky person... One slowly subsides. One does again the same thing one has forgotten one already did. One uses the same word three times in four sentences because it's been brought to the foreground but one somehow isn't aware of that. One writes inhibit instead of inhabit. It's all a dream. One becomes more consistent with non-conscious reality.

> And then it came to me, that feeling, the feeling that death was the truth, that this state of being alive was a sour chord played in death, a kind of dead end, tainted mutation, a freak and temporary warp and wart on death's resources, presently to be reabsorbed. That being alive was a lie, a kind of grotesque misuse of material—like a sculpture made of food—and that to be truthful I'd have to die.
> —"Boy Meets Death, Boy Falls in Love" (1999), *Hot and Cold* (powerHouse, 2001)

I've more than once had this eerie, almost mathematical, but comforting experience, when falling asleep, of disintegrating, and I realize as it's happening that it's dying, the experience of dying, but also that that straightforward subjection to physical laws (rather than all the psychological phenomena—emotions, etc.—which trick us into thinking we have agency) is reality.

> The waking world, consciousness, "life," is the dream;
> the falling asleep world, death, is the reality.
> —from *Untitled* (Merde : Press, 2018)

As this essay shows, the sense has recurred for me in inklings my whole life that being half asleep is the closest thing to reality, and now those inklings have coalesced. It's like love or religion. I'm surprised to find that when I'm feeling fear, worthlessness, self-disgust, which has always happened and is possibly worse now that I am almost seventy, remembering that I'm dreaming and a dream, the reconciliation of consciousness and the inanimate, of human birth and death relieves me of despair. A good epitaph would be "OUT OF CONTROL." Mmmm. The drowsy feeling the warm milk brings.

CHRONICLE

1. snow is falling in huge clumps
   and gravity seems depressing

2. engrave on tombstone:
   out of control

3. people are different
   from each other and
   can't communicate

4. whenever I learn that someone has read something by
   me I realize I haven't written what I thought I had

5. what is the difference between eyes opened and eyes
   closed

6. Poetry is what reminds you what it's like to live.

7. the thing concealed by
   everything mysterious
   is one's description of it

8. hounded by the desire
   to be realistic

9. I decided to let myself become
   this thing of rock and roll

10. seeing something through a window is unlike being on the other side of the window

11. The phenomena and ideas that are the most fascinating are, like Gödel's theorem, those that point to the realization that one can't understand the world because one is a part of it (the world) and so trying to encompass results only in noise, like feedback, like infinite mirroring, a thing looking at itself (which is impossible and only creates those jarring alarms). I resist authority; to live in serenity one has to accept one's subordination, give up trying to understand or control. This theme is everywhere. My wish to be God, which is hopeless. (All damned religions and spiritual programs are about accepting one's subservience, about humility before incomprehensible powers over oneself.)

12. ENABLED BY THE FORM OF THE TONGUE

Way interesting how Daniel Mendelsohn's description (*Waiting for the Barbarians*, p. 168, etc.) of how Horace achieves his effects in his *Odes* demonstrates that one's given language and its syntax, etc., can be exploited for its specific means (which may differ from other languages, or even be unique) to make supreme literature. So, whether or not one's language reveals or creates elements of one's worldview (like, say, the supposedly debunked idea that the Inuit have forty words for snow), it does enable, or at least provide efficient congenial means to achieve extraordinary literary effects. (In Horace it's how he exploits Latin's indifference to certain word-sequencing in sentences to compose poems that are full of events that the reader has to order him- or herself, naturally making assumptions—secretly designed or allowed by Horace—until finally they all get ordered and fall into place as describing a particular situation only at the end of the poem when its object/subject emerges... It's like a detective story enabled by the form of the literature's tongue. ...Maybe similar to the deliberately scrambled-time movie narratives popularized in the U.S. by Tarantino.)

13. Undergoing that semi-dying of the drift into dozing mid-afternoon and suddenly it feels dreadful and, like last words, I feel the panicked thought, "I wanna go back!"

14. Fucking *time*. Now I feel like I'm at the end of my life, when from forty-five or so I've been wrestling with not being young, all the way till now, when I've become old. All the past looks different, as if it's a story. No, not "the past," but just my life, because, being old, it's essentially over now. (Something is only a story if it has an ending.) I have pity (and sorrow) for the person I've been, and dread and regret and fear and pain for how I've behaved towards others. But it's like having been assigned a role, a story, because that's the mind's nature. I had and did a lot and I didn't have or do a lot. But the striving does seem poignant now that it's over, because none of it had any meaning and I usually thought it did, no matter how I might assume otherwise at times. It was all uncontrollable drives that have

shifted and altered over time till there's not much left, and that's all.

15. Duchamp's *3 Standard Stoppages* is an embodiment, a pure materialization, of the act of art in that it presents a fragment of a universe, that universe which can be extrapolated from the fragment, in the way that a work of the imagination is a communication from another reality (being another person). Also is a perfect example of the only thing I think of as consistently advisable for an artist, which is to find the underlying, previously unconscious, whole conceptual stage or foundations—premise(s)—enabling or unconsciously supporting one's artistic acts, and subvert that, question it, speak from that refreshing doubt, rather, beyond conventions and habits. Like the trained animal that suddenly realizes it can simply leave the yard. (Or else the opposite: find the outermost surface of experience and speak from there—like Andy Warhol or David Trinidad.) (Which is actually the same thing.) (The number of keys is upright infinity twice.)

16. You don't have to understand something to learn from it. In art you can misread or have an ignorant take on works or artists that interest you, and still draw productive implications and make interesting art influenced by those works or artists. (This is wrapped up in all the retrospection, or looking back at my works of 40-50 years ago, I've been doing or that has been being done to me ((40th anniversary *Blank* double-disc; Kyle Void and Merde : Press; White Columns exhibit of my small press history; "remastered" Ernie Stomach's

uh)) and how I have lately found more acceptable and respectable than I once did the earliest work, say from 1967-1970, for having an interest of its own partly for the very way it was heavily influenced by work I didn't understand very well, like Dylan Thomas, 2nd gen NY School poets... And also Proust's admonition ((via Elstir in *Search* I believe)) that it's ignoble and cramped, self-defeating, to be ashamed of one's earlier, perhaps less interesting or less sophisticated works, because one can only have gotten to anything more interesting by having passed through the prior stages.) Baudelaire being influenced by Poe (Baudelaire in this case being the superior poet) reinforces the idea, because if a man as subtle as Baudelaire could think Poe a great poet he would have to have been talking about something that gained in translation, translation into Baudelaire... (I conjecture without being able to read French.) In a way, this is the norm, in fact: when young, and often much later, artists often only go on intuition—their own sensibilities—in reading the art of their times (and before). It's the norm that it's a surprise when they eventually discover the actual intentions and methods of the artists they admire. Rather, they're responding to what they take in ignorance, like, say, almost all the "Cubists" subsequent to Picasso and Braque and Gris, though many of them, like Delaunay—and tons of artists who weren't in Paris—had to go on a lot of conjecture and personal inclinations in figuring out how to keep up with the new advances, but made worthwhile work despite not well understanding their inspirers. (Eventually I happen to come across another example in talk about Cézanne in *Brooklyn Rail* for

June 2020 between John Elderfield and Terry Winters: "John Elderfield: This is probably as good a moment as any to say that, while both Picasso and Matisse said that Cézanne was the father of us all, like all artistic fathers, he is not responsible for what his children do. In fact, what the children did was, of course, very different from what Cézanne did. Certainly, the common understanding that Cézanne's principal impact was on the development of Cubism is hardly supportable. Working on this exhibition, I have felt even more that associating Cézanne with the increasingly reductive geometric painting of the early part of the twentieth century is a wrong understanding of his importance. His increasingly proximate views of rocks seem to take you to the epicenter of his art in so vividly binding their depicted surfaces to the literal surfaces of his paintings. That constituted the great Cézannean revolution. Not that Cézanne made Cubism possible. / Winters: It was almost a non-sequitur. In the same sense that Pop-art was a non-sequitur following Jasper Johns.")

17. Boswell, in trying to plumb Johnson for his biography, would intrusively overreach, as when he asked him, "What would you do if you were locked in a tower with a newborn baby?" Johnson replied, "I have no intention of answering such an inept question."

18. immersed in one's interior

19. The poetic satisfaction of receiving someone's requested selfie sex photo. How it's about dominating, being submitted to, but also the picture itself. The

picture a kind of symbol of itself. (I think the desire to sexually dominate, receive submission, comes from insecurity ((as well as the obvious hope for instant gratification)), the need for relief from doubt about how much, or in what way, one is wanted by the person in question. It's selfish possibly, but for many in both roles ((dominant, submissive)) a welcome escape from continuous doubt about what's wanted or expected of oneself, about what's best behavior, in a given sexual encounter.)

20. It's people who do things as subtly interesting and well-made as Kyle Void has done that get mocked by petty squares like John Seabrook.

21. You can talk to yourself because you need to get your own attention, like if you're distracted but there's something you need to do that takes focus. (Another reason is you're imagining, you're foreseeing communicating something—either writing it or saying it—and, undergoing the act in your head, you unconsciously do it aloud.)

22. Sudden feeling of exalted well-being. I'm bathed and on a New York street, it's springtime and a taxi is coming for me.

23. snowy night in New York City [it's not snowy nor nighttime but I'm reading Joe Brainard]

24. "'It won't get any worse!' he would say, and smile with his upper lip alone." (p. 4, *Sakhalin Island*)—

Chekhov's way of describing that facial expression that, as enacted by Quine, I've mentioned in a few places, *Tramp* for instance: "There was a thing Bob would do. Instead of smiling, he would just stretch his lips across his teeth in a cursory sign for 'smile.' His eyes wouldn't change at all, just his mouth for a moment. It was actually friendly—a signal that he was not unwilling to expend the energy to give a little conventional reassurance." It's fun to compare the way different writers describe the same thing. Chekhov notices so much he doesn't have time for more than a brief sentence to get across what it takes me three medium-length sentences, but his says as much. (Though Chekhov's "migrating"-into-Siberia peasant's pseudo-smile is grim and ironic, not encouraging like Bob's.) Partly because he's being specific—the gesture happens in an active scene, rather than as an abstracted tendency, the way I was doing. But, "There was a thing Bob would do: smile with his upper lip alone" is better anyway.

25. I would like something to happen for me on the water. I would love for there to be a Richard Hell Landing. Some kind of address on a river.

26. What if all that's left is a form of nostalgia: a longing for a greater degree of innocence? It feels something like that sometimes now, that the only material I have is the past—not the past itself actually, but me in a previous state—when I still believed there was something realistically to aspire to. When I assumed I was pure enough to achieve something.

27. The older I get the less I know, or, rather, what happens is you discover that the things you hid from yourself about yourself out of fear and low character or else that you believed you'd naturally overcome in time are permanent and fatal. (I'm not the person I thought I was.)

28. I felt the process of going crazy when I was standing at the sink this morning. I was hating myself so much, hating what I've done to people, abandoning them, that I suddenly felt this wave of fear that people were trying to kill me—roots paranoia. I could feel how paranoia, at least in some cases, is rooted in self-loathing and guilt. I could feel it tip into insanity.

29.   LATE LIFE BAD SUNDAY

> Music seems damp.
> It's too cold in this room to put
> it on I think on my striped couch.
> Smudged windowpanes the sun
> struggles through would shine
> on acid, but now, not.
> Are those windows alive?

*

LATE LIFE

> Forty years ago when I
> was a junkie I craved
> something to believe in.

> The feeling has returned
> but now
> I know I won't find it.

30. Noise is more like existence so it would seem noise art would be best. Though I guess one's particular contribution is to the cacophony. I've done my part. I only even wrote this by force.

31. It seems odd how forms of thought, as can be seen in vintage non-fiction (or other humanistic analysis) date. The way cultures view human reality is constantly mutating and it's almost impossible to live outside of those influences. One just has to hope one's been born into a culture that might permit networks of thought (minds) that are interesting and have some capacity to endure.

32. All this uniqueness. (Reading Roth—dead this week at 85—on plane to Portugal, *Everyman* as it happens, and thinking, as he describes a person or two, how similar we all are, how delusional it is to treat human individuality as meaningful, but then it's true we're each unique no matter how insignificantly.) (Reminds me of that Bill Knott poem (("Poem," though I saw it somewhere printed as "Another Cold War Poem")): "So what if you lived only / One second longer / Than we / Did: to us / You will always be known as the Survivor.") [Found in *Selected and Collected Poems*, 1977, from Sun] (Elsewhere noted how people can't communicate because each is a separate world. The impassable gulf between each and the similarity of all are equally true. Is it that

art—like the Roth book—is what combines the two?)

Knott's perhaps best-known poem "Death," that gave the title to his posthumous FSG *Selected Poems*, goes, "Going to sleep, I cross my hands on my chest. / They will place my hands like this. / It will look as though I am flying into myself." ...The A. Poulin, Jr. translation of Rilke includes these lines from the first Duino Elegy, "[...] Throw the emptiness in / your arms out into that space we breathe; maybe birds / will feel the air thinning as they fly deeper into themselves." ...Which is a poetry similar to Bill.

33. "Then he walked ceremoniously to the head of the grave, stood there a moment to think his thoughts, and, angling the shovel downward a little, let the dirt run slowly out. Upon landing on the wood cover of the coffin, it made the sound that is absorbed into one's being like no other." [Roth, *Everyman*, p. 58] That last sentence seemed so strong I wanted to note it down, but on second thought I realized it was probably not true, but false, hyperbolic. A few pages later I was thinking again, that it wasn't even true for Roth himself—it just produced the effect he wanted. And I thought, does that make it OK, as art's lies that open us to the truth (as per Picasso, etc.)? Maybe so.

Jesus, the sordidness (which is actually a Roth way of putting it—the unselfconsciousness of saying "sordidness"—the kind of wording that David Foster Wallace didn't mind writing too) of reading his *Everyman* now that I see where it's really going. It makes me sick, reel to see. But the twisted mirror reality to go along with Kyle Void and the strange Pessoa book (in which Pessoa is watercolor-illustrated in my pose as on *Blank* cover, revealing his chest on which is written "YOU MAKE ME _____") ... What is happening, everything breaking up into phenomena switching attributes with each other? Being the Ancient Mariner again. And like my life is writing its story, its aesthetic culmination in abjection and trivial soulless horror. (Moments after I write that I find the stone has come off of the ring Sheelagh gave me when we were separating.)

34. My whole life is going to sleep (declining towards death).

35. Sitting in aisle airplane seat with three different screens viewable (one to the left forward; one to the right; and one to the right forward)—two movies and an animated TV show—while I'm reading... Each separate world. So's the seat back. All these ridiculous clumsy incongruous tunnels of slightly more self-consistent phenomena.

36. Maybe I could just write separate scenes and they could do as they will. Getting old, betraying love, some cartoon, Ernie, Theresa, an amoeba. Looking at someone surreptitiously and imagining she's someone else but stopping before crying. Like a stupid hopeless sad sunset of the scenes. "Don't the sun look..."—a book, illuminated book—no message but itself and something to do; justifying oneself as per Borges. I think I have his sympathy.

37. My memory always bad. It occurs to me that I've probably been absolutely everywhere there is but I just don't remember any of it very well. It's hazy and all runs together and a lot of it disappears. Maybe this is also true of everybody else. Merciful.

38. I reveled in an alienation when I was young, expressed by Theresa as "I am not human," that embarrasses me now for its self-drama and a sense that it's actually an expression of timidity, fear of engagement, but the alienated feeling has never gone away, only now I experience it as frustration and even bitterness (embarrassing) about all the pet180ss of living as a humanist, when humans are so impure, so molded by evolutionary forces to behave in ways we don't even recognize, much less acknowledge, much less understand. I guess it's a labyrinthine path because I also remember first noticing the word humanism—I'm almost sure it was in an interview with Bill Knott—and being excited and inspired by the concept (after initial confusion—as I was confused by the word "sexism" when I first read it in the *Village Voice*). I wonder how my auto-didacticism (or however you'd put it) shows. You wouldn't think that leaving school after age 16 would make that much difference for someone as interested in thinking and learning as I have been. But I think it does show. I think it's affected my prose style, which might have benefitted from some more formal study and guidance. But it sometimes makes my prose feel more alive too.

39. The brief, pleasant feeling, immediately upon smoking a joint, of walking around naked in a warm pudding.

40. Reading Chekhov's *Sakhalin Island*, and an endnote [p. 330, regarding p. 33] refers to "a favorite book" of Chekhov's since childhood, and "book" there in that context, as the category (rather than "novel" or "of poems" or "biography" or such) moves me, feels magic and inspiring. It was a favorite *book* of his since childhood. (In fact, the book, as the note states, was *Frigate "Pallada"* (1858), a nonfiction account of an around-the-world exploration on which its author, I. A. Goncharov, travelled as secretary.) I don't know what it is about the concept of producing a good book, book as book, irrespective of genre or form, that feels so magical to me, like reassuring and redemptive—book as a means of delivering information that perfectly integrates intellectual and emotional content with its material form—when I know from experience that the fantasy is more specific, namely that poetry would be involved as well as whatever the effective attractions for the eye and hand—and that it's a vague dream that I've had forever without taking it anywhere (though perhaps Theresa and *Psychopts*, two collaborations, come closest...*Weather* worked pretty well too...).

The dream of the Book.

41. What is this thing where I just can't accept life??? That I can't affirm anything because I am not convinced I know anything, I am not convinced anything is knowable by the likes of me (us). The oddness of standing

at the kitchen sink and seeing the gleaming, squirming rope of water plunging from the mouth of the faucet and remembering how that beauty was once enough to ground and please me, while now I'm too disillusioned and I can only see it as something I've been conditioned to, or that I'm biologically inclined to, like. What the fuck?

42. Strange—just read a sentence that ended like so, "[...] grew up on the Upper East Side, where she felt she was an outcast," and it gave me this feeling of power and inspiration. What is that? I need to feel like an outcast to be strong and accomplish anything?

43. No free will: Spinoza, Schopenhauer, Nietzsche, Borges... Jesus, it's like it's not even controversial, while at the same time it's completely taken for granted as false. I'd say 99.999% of people fully believe in free will (believe that their worldview and behavior are ultimately controlled by themselves).

44. The strangeness of viewing a moving picture where some monotonously repetitive (but interesting?) activity (blow job?) continues for a long time, some minutes, so that one becomes fully engaged in observing the action (as opposed to orienting oneself in relation to the visual) and it continues until—snip—a cut to a radically different angle the same distance from the action/focal point and just as fully exposing it (such as a direct full profile followed by a high angle). So the mind suddenly has to reach for a purpose or interpretation of the juxtaposition of the two

shots, the addition of the second shot. It feels like some kind of dramatic or at least significant revelation of the essential power of filmmaking. Also like an abyss: suddenly the world becomes so much bigger and more complex—for what reason? One demands that the change be justified, that if such a radical act is to be performed it must carry its weight and be equally radically meaningful.

45. Essay about Robert Crumb as suggested by how women are immune to his genius. Or at least Katherine and Eva are. As we were discussing at a table outside the Bait & Hook on 14th St. the other day. They insist that women don't care for him. I've had this debate before but it still surprises me, while on reflection I understand what they mean, how they could feel that way. (Undoubtably #metoo makes it easier to understand.) Then I remember Melody seems completely warm about him (an old friend of hers), and then, of course, there's his significant other (Aline) and Dian Hanson at Taschen. But to write an essay about how I want to defend Crumb or sympathize with him while I still recognize what offends Katherine and co. about him (he is criticized for using racial stereotypes too). This could have blended into it that remark from yesterday about responding to women passersby on the street—entailing the ability, increased by my advanced age I think, to view them simultaneously as two separate entities: their erotic signals and zones and powers alongside their separate personal being as it is when divorced from all sexual, erotic aspects. But the main thing is that his essence (apart from his comics-art genius,

command of the medium) is how he admits all, not to affirm his dicey areas, but not to pretend they don't exist, either, and that's rare and important. It wouldn't excuse him causing anyone harm, but he's not causing anyone harm—he's encouraging by example honesty above safety and complacency and self-satisfaction.

- how I was mortified to see, years later, how I wrote about the women in the *Spin* "Search for the Soul of Rock and Roll" piece (ca 1986)
- the strange thing where Katherine told me she was writing an essay on "beauty" and I was eating it up, the idea, and we conversed for a few sentences until I realized she was working entirely on the assumption that the use of the word "beauty" unqualified refers to human/social standards for feminine appearance (which preoccupies her, obviously, and maddens and frustrates her)
- to really be frank, willing to be wrong, in effort to claw down to the foundations of thinking about how I think about women...
- [later date] I felt I came upon a female equivalent to the Crumb issue in the case of Avital Ronell's behavior with her young gay male grad student advisee. How she's creepy but it's possible to have empathy for it because it's a deprived intellectual's behavior with sex objects once the professor's so powerful he or she can get away with acting on their poor idea of romantic/sexual relationships.

46. What if "whore" or "slut" were a compliment? I can feel it.

47. Reading analysis of Kafka's extraordinarily powerful and creepy "Crossbreed" short-short story about a "Cat-Lamb"—a pet that's part cat and part lamb—and find the analysis is founded in Judaic mythology and the Old Testament, a tradition that's so obscure, obsolete that it's pretty much inaccessible, certainly not effective for its underlying power or pattern, and it makes me think of the way relations between men and women and all the old existing assumptions about their relations are no longer shared in the culture and it undermines big swaths of literature, renders them irrelevant. It's a phenomenon—that of dying cultural tenets and assumptions—significant to Borges, its poignancy—the idea of the last old god left alive... (Though it's also true that this can be cyclical—if the culturally outdated writing is good enough, it can eventually return to acceptance when the morally defective parts are so old-hat that they aren't provocative anymore.)

47. The variety of things is interesting; it's boring for the same reason. No conclusions, only struggle.

48. I love the smell of my sweaty balls. It makes me think of beautiful brown rain clouds filling the sky. Why is rain so consoling and improving? It probably has to do with the seriousness of life. You know, beautiful sadness, isolation, fertility, what all. Just like my balls.

50. AFTER EZRA POUND

Tawny rain clouds fill the sky;
The fragrance of my sweaty balls.

51. Recently I can't stand to read studies of literature and writers or painting and painters, music/musicians, etc., even regarding me, myself, because they so consistently exaggerate their subjects' importance and influence. Everybody is a major force of his or her era, if not more, whether acknowledged by others or not. It's a waste of time and boring. Even the greatest (Proust, Dante, Shakespeare) are just good artists—why does that make them more important than everybody else? Nothing matters very much. We're all what we have to be.

52. It occurs to me that when I get bored I tend to try two things, either go for a walk or look at a periodical. It would be interesting to make a movie that was a person taking a walk in a magazine.

53. The way my motivation seems to be decreasing as I get old (though it's not as if I haven't noticed ennui and lack of motivation before)... I'm not interested in idiosyncrasies of the human anymore. I don't think we're interesting except to the extent that I can recognize hidden or profound new (to me) such idiosyncrasies. I just think we're freak mutations without further meaning. I don't trust my senses or my powers of analysis or understanding. Because I'm a poor human. What is there to do? I mean, literally: what's worth doing? Not even pleasure works. Because it gets tired. The only reliable happiness or feeling of achievement is to be

loved and admired. Worshipped preferably. I remember how it made me happy to see in Will's journals—Will a generous-spirited and good person—how all he wanted is to be worshipped ("I'M MEAN AND AFRAID AND I WANT YOU TO WORSHIP ME."). It made it feel less shameful. I guess that's another appeal of religion—you're told that God loves you no matter what.

54. Another dead person. Almost anybody you can talk about is dead.

55. It is a little eerie the parallels between Richard Prince's artistic history and sensibility and mine. Too extensive and tangled to detail, but what just brought it to mind was seeing and reading the top (bio note/photo) area of my Criterion top ten list. And the parallel is that I see the person and read his paragraph bio note, and I get this sudden feeling of inspiration (which I've really been lacking lately) that comes from thinking, "Oh, that's strong. What would be fun to see added to his list of accomplishments?" Like that feeling of aesthetically shaping one's bio (one's behavior and goals) being a most welcome stimulus to work. I'm given the persona (the way RP describes himself needing to in order to start off on a project, the way doing a "hippie" drawing was an assignment he gave himself, a persona he deliberately adopted), and then that's the creative act: conceiving how that person(a) would behave, what do next (as I took on identities of Ernie, Theresa, Hell)... And over and over odd touchpoints of me and Richard: we're born the same year (1949), cowboys, mopar, pornography, being funny... But... It's really an

illusion. No one would look at our separate bodies of work and see resemblance. His is also so much fuller while also being well focused. It's his achievement, like all the best artists, to make people see the world as it is organized through the lens of him, and recognize it, feel that they live there too.

56. "On the other hand..." (Signature phrase...) A subject that I am interested in and think about and would like to sort out in an essay is something along the lines of "Is younger better?" But it goes all over the landscape to get to such as "Is it shameful to want fame?" (It's rare to stay very famous without wanting to?) (Makes me think of that interview with John Ashbery where he said he starts to feel uncomfortable if he hasn't seen his name in the media lately. And I felt a little relieved to see that—like the Will thing about wanting to be worshipped. But it turned out the Ashbery interview was a hoax! Ha ha... Though, in my defense—I may like to be known to people, but I will not behave unnaturally to get there...) On one hand I feel like what's usually thought of as human life is actually only human life from the ages of 17 to 35 or some such, because that's the period when we are our sharpest and most capable (and have the most appeal for advertisers!). But the way it's assumed, "taken for granted," that the preoccupations and skills and values and preferences of the very young are superior or more advanced... Offends me and seems mistaken. You know, the way a person in their fifties can be dismissed as unworthy because he or she doesn't understand what Snapchat is. The toxic mixture, in our time, of extreme identity

politics (trigger warnings and such) (the idea that you shouldn't write about people that you don't resemble) and ("on the other hand") the unexamined assumption that "success" is to have designed a killer app... Ugh...

57. Another subject: The possibility that among the reasons that suicide is common among the elderly is that you've lived long enough for your fatal flaw to get undeniably exposed.

58. I was just looking at the Kier illustrated edition of *The Voidoid* and feeling happy and relieved. Well, first, it's such a nicely done edition, the graphics so good, and design... all the signed limited/Japanese-bound copies with individual cover drawings... But, emphatically, my main takeaway the quality of the written thing. I feel like I made there at the age of 23 a work that found a form for the values in writing and the view of things I had then and it was actually sophisticated. I feel like I was able to find a form that corresponded to how reality felt to me, which is the most a writer can hope to do, or at least a sect of writer I respect. Also, it's like an ouroboros in that it intensely/vividly/jokingly presents the way I feel now, in 2018. It's funny, after all the years I considered it a kind of crude eccentricity. Not that I was embarrassed—I did put out three editions of it over the years. The Josh/Kier one feels so good and right to me now and incidentally reaffirms for me the worthiness of continuously, when I see the possibility, improving any old works that have any value to me at all. ("On the other hand" I know that

it could easily happen that the next time I pick it up I'll be mortified by it.)

59. Found a Primo Levi I hadn't read, *The Truce*, when I'm in a condition that it's the only kind of material I can take seriously. And there is this finality of despair, no matter how he pushes to survive, that underlies everything because once it's experienced, it's final; that's the essence of the phenomenon: "We returned to the train with heavy hearts. We had felt no joy in seeing Vienna destroyed and the Germans defeated: pity, rather; not compassion but a broader pity, which mingled with our own wretchedness, with the heavy, looming sensation of an irreparable and ultimate evil, present everywhere, hidden like a cancer in the bowels of Europe and the world, the seed of future harm."

60. You don't have to be that smart to be too smart for your own good.

61. In a way, some of the strength of my writing about art/movies/books comes from my not having an education, because I have to find out for myself what's interesting and why—for instance my piece on Bresson and my piece on Picabia, which are about the experience of being educated by the art itself... (I remember how exciting it was to suddenly notice when looking at a Cézanne painting in the Met that this is where Cubism came from. I'd had no idea before that... It wouldn't have been the same if I learned it from another party.)

62. What are celebrities? After attending with Katherine the Courtney Love evening benefitting Basilica last night. I'm jealous of celebrities, of people who can behave for a public in a way that makes them popular or at least fascinating. But I don't like being in the same room with them. People who are always "on." But I want to be worshipped! The whole thing is depressing. Something in me thinks only celebrities have succeeded in life. While I also despise them (Courtney) (and of course know that the huge preponderance of admirable people are never publicly recognized). I know that not only are dubious traits associated with the ability to attain celebrity (though of course not always—take, say, Einstein), but that, as a rule, if you weren't already a creep, great fame will make you one. But who am I to pronounce people "creeps"? Is it defensive? The whole thing of fame is confusing. Keats, the deserving archetype of the sensitive, passionate and compassionate poet, seemingly unselfconsciously wanted it; it was assumed to be certification of his poetic achievements. But what is this scary culture here and now where celebrity is everyone's preoccupation? Or is it humanly eternal—earlier ones were warriors and royals and saints...? Warhol (article due for *Gagosian* in two weeks).

63. Speaking of Einstein, apparently he was another "free will skeptic." Says philosophy professor Gregg D. Caruso (in a debate with Daniel Dennett):

> Consider the case of Albert Einstein. He too was a free-will skeptic who believed that his scientific

accomplishments were not of his own making. In a 1929 interview in *The Saturday Evening Post*, he said: "I do not believe in free will ... I believe with Schopenhauer: we can do what we wish, but we can only wish what we must." He goes on to add: "My own career was undoubtedly determined, not by my own will but by various factors over which I have no control." He concludes by rejecting the idea that he deserves praise or credit for his scientific achievements: "I claim credit for nothing. Everything is determined, the beginning as well as the end, by forces over which we have no control."

64. I was just reading *Rabbit Duck* when I saw in my imagination the pretty image of a butterfly on my girlfriend's upraised anus. (It also kind of sounds like something A. Warhol could have done in spare goofy elegant ink-drawing in the 1950s. Also brings to mind Jim Carroll/Edwin Denby story from *Forced Entries* I just recently saw cited, about Denby and de Kooning walking down the street and a butterfly attacks de Kooning's eyes—which, incidentally, I think may have been entirely invented by Carroll taking off from a story Denby told in his essay "The Thirties" [collected in *Dance Writings and Poetry* ((Yale: 1998))] about being told by de Kooning that he ((de Kooning)) had once seen André Breton across the street in New York "making peculiar gestures in front of his face" and it was the Surrealist fighting off a butterfly attack.)

65. Good description [by Emily Flake in *New Yorker*] of an adult returning, much later, to visit provincial

hometown: "I've been gone for so much longer than I was here, and yet it feels like walking back into a room where they've been keeping the truth for you."

66. Word artwork:

It's over.

67. New feeling: I picked up three small books in succession that I'd forgotten I had: a very thin book of poems by Terry Ork (William Terry Drake) published by his friend soon after Terry died (2007); *Corpers* (poems, 1981, published by its author, dedicated "to Richard Meyers") by old brief-running-buddy long-dead Amy Pollé; and Jamie MacInnis's *Hand Shadows* (1974) (the one of the three who wasn't a friend of mine—never heard of her till years after she disappeared; the book an Adventures in Poetry side-stapled mimeo type thing)—and each in succession for the first time I can remember, as if they were linked to or even embodied, essences, were possessed by and conveyed the people who were their authors. It felt almost holy, to use a super-charged word. I felt them and was confusedly under influence of emotion. I didn't know books could be people, purely, in that way. It made me happy and glad. It's true, I thought. It happened in cobwebs but it was as true and real—the presence of the people inherent in those books for me—as any other "direct" experience, simple life undergone.

68. Baudelaire in a passage about how he'd come to realize the error and futility of working up a system

describing how things are—what the universe is—(because you just have to continuously, exhaustingly revise or replace the system as experience renders the prior version incomplete and obsolete): "[...] I proudly resigned myself to modesty: I was content to feel." "I proudly resigned myself to modesty"! Ha ha. But a good, advisable move. Waste of time to try to figure it all out, as seductive as the attempt is. [*Baudelaire as Literary Critic*, from "Exposition Universelle of 1855" (pp. 80-81)]

69. Another somewhat reassuring way to look at it: I will return to a greater intelligence when I die.

70. song: "I Wish You Loved Me"—can't go wrong

71. Even in case of scientist Lévi-Strauss, one loves him as much for his point of view, his sensibility, as for his intelligence or his ideas.

72. title: *Real Direct*

73. What if the meaning of the world is that framed poetry-flier drawing by Joe Brainard (Ted Berrigan & Harry Fainlight at Café La Mamma [sic] on Mother's Day, 1964) I have hanging on my office wall now?

74.   I think my mind might be going
         and at this moment I don't terribly
         mind. One thing it does is incline me
         to use the same word in possibly
         too close proximity to itself.

> But I like those two "mind"s. Their
> meaning is different, for one thing. I
> mean, in this case, I guess
> it's a statement in itself.
> And it's not too hard to fix if I want.
> (Is that too many "too"s?)
> Also, losing one's mind is consistent
> with the universe (everything). It's not
> like a loss, really: Who's in charge—
> the universe or us? It's the people,
> like me, who think too much
> who were mistaken all along.
> That's really not
> where I intended to go with this.
> Such sweeping statements are foolish
> unless they're funny. I'll call it funny.

75. "Frozen-faced introverts dedicated to chaos" (!) being what I think Ralph Ellison was just quoted as saying about early bebop drummers... [Ken Burns's *Jazz* series]

76. Idea of a fantasy/sci-fi novel, or story more likely, that would investigate a world where everyone had the capacity to kill anyone else without it being at all possible to be discovered as the perp. Or somehow looks at the idea of what would happen if people could kill with the certainty that they'd not be identified as the murderer.

77. I think suicide comes when the shame of being oneself, of having one's failings, becomes too great to even hope to be able to alleviate at all by describing

it, confessing it. That level of aloneness. And there's no reply, or worse, to confessing that nothing is interesting anymore. It's an insult to whomever one admits it to.

78. I'm not innocent enough to find clouds and trees beautiful anymore. Maybe the ocean, but that's not just "beauty," it's impenetrability.

79. The human truth of the universe is incomprehensibility.

80. It's always been the same! I feel exactly as I did at 21 or 22 on Elizabeth Street, lying in bed alone staring at the wall in hopeless self-lacerating despair and emptiness (*The Voidoid*), the eternal "thank you, I'm sorry" cycle regarding my relations to everyone (women, mostly) (my need to be wanted by numbers of them whether I especially cared about them or not) tormenting me with self-loathing, paralyzed. It's never been any different! The words to "Blank Generation" are still the case! The confusion, and desire to escape, and the guilt and self-disgust and regret but that's never enough to change me, but rather always leads to the ultimate "I don't care" regarding consequences, regarding other standards, regarding arduous paths to any improvement (regarding my own problems!!!). What is this psychological condition? All right, "solipsism," except I don't want to be in myself, but I don't have the energy to build up the power and speed to crash out of it... The unpleasant self-centeredness, failures of kindness. How and why did I end up like that, like this? I know I wasn't unkind as a child.

81. Am I the only one who does it? Reads everything in partial hope of answers, for clues about how to live or how to frame life so it's more bearable? What to look at to not be sad? It's so embarrassing. Where's my substance? Reading Anne Carson's translations of Euripides, specifically *Alkestis*, and speech after speech I have my gravitation towards application of the points of view (expressed as characters in the play) to myself (in other words identification with the character, as vulgar an approach to literature as that may be) undermined by how the next speaker is just as vivid and convincing (identifiable with) in completely rebutting and contradicting the first. I have to say it's a brilliant technique—great basis for tragedy. (Is this what they mean by dialectical?) Maybe I should do that to "dramatize" my condition—divide it into speaking characters. (Also occurs to me that this Euripides-Greek-tragedy technique recalls my thought about Shakespeare that every character gets full dignity and dimensionality, as if a given play could have been about a character in it who only has two lines, and also the sense that all of them carry on after the play is over ((the ones left alive))).

82. Now reading biography of the magisterially human Claude Lévi-Strauss. It's as depressing as it is impressive and admirable. I mean he is (depressing, etc.)—as followed in such detail in the long book. The depressing part is how intelligent and capable he is. I don't mind how interesting his mind is, or how soulful he is, which is to say those things are what I love, but his intelligence and equilibrium and capabilities are painful

for how I wish I had those qualities. At the same time I feel like, regarding his extreme intelligence, I can grasp enough of the complexities of his most advanced scientific thought to feel they're not alien to me, not inaccessible—but it's an extreme strain to comprehend the most subtle of their forms and implications, when he is at his most abstract and/or advanced, spinning ideas. I think that intelligence, from the average to the highest, is essentially the same, it just has fewer or more dimensions. Everybody is still searching for and perceiving patterns (which is what the intelligence does), and even perceiving the same ones, it's just that the most intelligent can hold more of a given one in his or her head at once, like playing three-dimensional chess rather than two-dimensional. It's not a meaningful achievement though—everyone still has the same problems. Just as the same goes for physical achievement. Good athletes don't have better lives. None of it matters.

83. Last night saw *Joker* (Todd Phillips) and I'm semi-inclined to write a piece defending it in the face of the contempt of liberal intellectuals (a group which normally I'd have to agree includes me) because, though I didn't exactly think it was a "good" movie, I felt it, and I thought it was valid, and seriously interesting. As a work of art it was not exactly high level, if ingenious and intelligent in many ways, and it was inconsistent—parts worked a lot better than others—but the turgid grotesquerie and despair and squalor pictured was worthy of portrayal, being an aspect of the human condition—including inevitably the human condition in

society, because humans are social—that's not often captured in art, and it was portrayed well, if maybe not with the profundity of Greek tragedy. It was as good as many first-rate noirs. And the connections to *Taxi Driver* and *King of Comedy* were interesting. *King of Comedy* was a better work, but *Joker* almost rivaled *Taxi Driver* in a few ways, including how, in *Joker*, the audience was given more of a feeling for how the character came to be in his condition than in *Taxi Driver*. *Joker* was the Grand Guignol comic book version, but I like comic books. The movie outrages humanists because it, however clumsily and perhaps inadvertently, shows empathy for hopeless nihilism. And of course this is an especially tender point in the Trump era. (I didn't buy absolutely everything Joaquin pulled, but there was brilliant acting in many scenes: the dancing, especially in the scene on those outdoor steps; the confrontation with the mayor; and then the brilliant perversion of Andy Kaufman in the ultimate talk-show scene. Also the play with standup was inspired, both the style of the generic comics and the complexity of what Phoenix did/said in his routine(s)—that joke about how when he was a kid and would claim he was going to be a comic everyone laughed at him, but "nobody's laughing now!" was beyond beyond...)

84. Guilt is such an ignoble emotion. I used to never feel it and I was proud of that, thinking my freedom from it was a virtue, a kind of frankness about life, but I think the heroin helped. Now I'm crippled by it. And that's shameful in itself.

85. As the coronavirus spreads and meanwhile I've already been in mood of the ephemerality of all ("Falling Asleep," etc.), I have a funny reaction to my new favorite picture frame-job—Godlis's "Closing Time" photo of barren, littered, black-and-white CBGB interior sometime around 4:00 AM in 1977—which is one of the first pictures I found rich in power to give me my life (without nostalgia), in that I look at it now and, because of the pandemic, it becomes weaker and more random, shifts towards becoming a reminder of human folly and arrogance and self-deception, because, rather than being a moment of rich associations, it is now merely more evidence of our meaninglessness, an example of the infinite quantity of meaningless gone time, this little pocket of human past, when "human" itself will soon be past.

86. Despite my appreciation of Lévi-Strauss's admiration for tribal societies (while he didn't over-romanticize them; his reservations regarding the human condition always present), and after a whole lifetime, it just now occurred to me that all the gods of humans were born of humans' terror at their fate. The "worshippers" weren't acting out of love and awe but out of fear, in hopes of propitiating whatever reigned. As far as I know, among world religions, only Buddhism is otherwise, and I think people give offerings to Buddha too...

87. The poignancy of people doing things, making the Venus of Willendorf, for instance.

88. foreshadowing

ACKNOWLEDGMENTS

Parts of this book have previously appeared in earlier forms in the following periodicals: *Blush, Brooklyn Rail, Caesura, F magazine, Lowbrow, Merde*. "Chronicle" first appeared as a chapbook published by F Publications in 2021.

Pages 81–82: From *Aurelia* by Gérard de Nerval in *Aurélia & Other Writings*, translated by Geoffrey Wagner, © Exact Change 1996. Published by Exact Change, Boston, and used by permission.

Pages 82–83: "They Dream Only of America" by John Ashbery, from *The Tennis Court Oath* © 1962, 1997, 2008 by John Ashbery. Published by Wesleyan University Press, Middletown CT, and used by permission.

Page 87: "Correspondences" by Charles Baudelaire, as published in *The Flowers of Evil*, translated by Keith Waldrop. Translation, Introduction, and Notes © 2006 by Keith Waldrop. Published by Wesleyan University Press, Middletown CT, and used by permission.

Pages 73–74: One photograph, and the same photograph reversed horizontally, from *The Pillar* by Stephen Gill. Copyright © 2019 Stephen Gill, used by permission of The Wylie Agency LLC.

RICHARD HELL is the author of several books of fiction, poetry, essays, notebooks, autobiography, and collaborations including *The Voidoid, Go Now, Godlike, Across the Years, Artifact, Hot and Cold, I Dreamed I Was a Very Clean Tramp, Massive Pissed Love, Wanna Go Out?* by Theresa Stern (with Tom Verlaine), and *Psychopts* (with Christopher Wool). He lives in New York.

CHRISTOPHER WOOL is widely regarded as one of the preeminent and most influential American painters of his generation. His work has been the subject of many museum exhibitions, including retrospectives at the Guggenheim Museum, New York, the Art Institute of Chicago and the Musee d'art Moderne, Paris.

This first edition comprises, in addition to the trade paperback, 41 clothbound copies signed by Richard Hell and Christopher Wool. Twenty-six are lettered A–Z, and 15, *hors commerce*, numbered 1–15.

What Just Happened
Copyright © Richard Hell, 2023
Images copyright © Christopher Wool, 2023
Photograph on pp. 73–74 from *The Pillar* by Stephen Gill,
copyright © 2019 Stephen Gill, used by permission of
The Wylie Agency LLC.

First Edition, 2023
ISBN 978-1-959708-00-1
LCCN: 2023930707

Winter Editions, Brooklyn, New York
wintereditions.net

WE books are typeset in Heldane, a renaissance-inspired serif designed by Kris Sowersby for Klim Type Foundry, and Zirkon, a contemporary gothic designed by Tobias Rechsteiner for Grilli Type. The typesetting was done by the editor. The cover was designed by Andrew Bourne with artwork by Christopher Wool. Printed and bound in Lithuania by BALTO Print.

Winter Editions

Emily Simon, IN MANY WAYS

Garth Graeper, THE SKY BROKE MORE

Robert Desnos, NIGHT OF LOVELESS NIGHTS, tr. Lewis Warsh

Richard Hell, WHAT JUST HAPPENED

Marina Tëmkina & Michel Gérard, BOYS FIGHT
[co-published with Alder & Frankia]

Helio Oiticica, SECRET POETICS, tr. Rebecca Kosick
[co-published with Soberscove Press]

Monica McClure, THE GONE THING

Claire DeVoogd, PATTERN ABYSS

Heimrad Bäcker, ON DOCUMENTARY POETRY, tr. Patrick Greaney

Ahmad Almallah, BORDER WISDOM